Reprints of Economic Classics

GOOD AND BAD TRADE

Also in

REPRINTS OF ECONOMIC CLASSICS

By SIR RALPH HAWTREY

The Art of Central Banking [1932]

A Century of Bank Rate [1939]

GOOD AND BAD TRADE

AN INQUIRY INTO THE CAUSES
OF TRADE FLUCTUATIONS

BY

R. G. HAWTREY

[1913]

WITH A NEW FOREWORD BY
THE AUTHOR 1961

REPRINTS OF ECONOMIC CLASSICS

Augustus M. Kelley · Publishers
NEW YORK 1970

First Edition 1913

(London: Constable & Company, 1913)

[1961?]

Reprinted 1962, 1970 by

AUGUSTUS M. KELLEY · PUBLISHERS

REPRINTS OF ECONOMIC CLASSICS

New York   New York   10001

By Arrangement With Constable & Company, Ltd.

. . . .

I S B N   0 678 00359 9

L C N   68 54735

PRINTED IN THE UNITED STATES OF AMERICA

by SENTRY PRESS, NEW YORK, N. Y. 10019

FOREWORD

I began writing this book in March, 1909, when the depression which followed the American crisis of 1907 was still unrelieved. I had become interested in the trade cycle when Joseph Chamberlain, in support of his case for tariff reform, compared British exports in 1903, a year of depressed trade and low prices, with those in 1873, a year of active trade and high prices. In 1909, I had been reading, in the twenty-year old Report of the Royal Commission on the Depression of Trade, of the complaints of various industries that they could not produce at a profit. It struck me that the extinction of profit could be explained if the price level fell in the interval between the incurring of costs and the sale of the product. And if traders borrowed at interest to finance profit-making business, they could pay a higher rate of interest when prices were rising and a lower rate when prices were falling. A falling price level makes a given market rate of interest more onerous, and a rising price level less so. Here, I thought, was a discovery, but I was disillusioned when I learnt from an economist friend that the principle was one already recognised, and had been expounded in Irving Fisher's work, *The Rate of Interest*.

But I was not discouraged, for at any rate its application to the explanation of the trade cycle would be new. It would explain why Bank rate was high at times of activity and low at times of depression.

The essence of this explanation to the trade cycle is on pp. 74-7: the lag of the rate of interest behind the change to rising or falling prices (p. 76), and the lag of the demand for hand-to-hand currency behind an expansion or contraction of credit (p. 75). The former lag accounts for the inherent instability of credit, while the latter accounts for the long period of the resulting oscillations, running usually to several years.

In this reasoning the efficiency of the rate of interest as an influence on borrowers was presupposed. It is the short-term rate of interest that the banks control, and its influence is felt principally by traders holding stocks of goods with borrowed money (pp. 62 and 185-6). The demand for capital outlay is equated to the available savings by the long-term rate (pp. 28-31), and the effect of a change in the short-term rate on the long-term rate is small (p. 53). Though "extensions, renewals or even repairs of plant can be postponed for a few weeks or a few months" (p. 64), a more substantial cause of fluctuations in the demand for capital outlay lies in what is now called the "acceleration principle", relating the demand for fixed capital to changes in the demand for finished products (p. 207).

Much of the analysis in this book employs the quantity theory of money in a crude form: a change in the income of a section of the community is assumed to mean a proportional change in its cash holding and *vice versa*. This served the purpose of exposition, and did not preclude account being taken of changes in velocity of circulation, e.g. the lag of the expansion of currency behind an increase in incomes (p. 75).

The book was not intended to be addressed especially to economists. I had read very little economics, and I did not want to complicate the statement of my theory by excursions into various controversies. And I was not able to address the financial world in its own language.

For example, the book exposed my ignorance of the
functions of bill-brokers (pp. 95, 103-4, 111-12, 132).
But I thought that the alternations of good and bad
trade must be of interest to all who concerned themselves with public affairs. The method of exposition
starting with a simplified model, and dropping the
simplifying hypotheses one after another, was intended
for this wider circle.

The concluding chapter is headed "Can Trade Fluctuations be prevented?" But is disavows the intention to
propose remedies.

In referring to Irving Fisher's plan for stabilising
the purchasing power of a system of token gold currencies, it notices the weak point of a price index number as the criterion of stability, in that it does not allow
for non-monetary causes of price changes, such as
scarcity of individual commodities (p. 258).

The criticism of the proposal of the Minority Report
of the Poor Law Commission in 1909 for using Government expenditure on public works, etc. to mitigate depressions, (pp. 259-61) failed to take account of the
possibility of the expenditure having a deliberately in-
flationary character.

The idea that "the great central banks of the world,
in whose hands the control rests, could agree together
to draw the reins a little tighter at times when an expansion of trade is in progress" (p. 268) foreshadows
one aspect of the Genoa Resolutions of 1922.

Soon after "Good and Bad Trade" appeared, F. H.
Keeling, an intellectual Socialist, reproached me with
having recommended reductions of wages. I disavowed
having made any such recommendation, though I had
contended that prompt and appropriate changes in
wages, upward as well as downward, would counteract

the injurious consequences of the cycle (pp. 265-7). Discussion elicited the fact that he was quite unaware that the supply of gold set a limit beyond which the wage level would cause increases of unemployment.

The book puts forward changes in the wage level as an alternative to "adopting an inconvertible paper currency, subject to a system of banking control which would effectively prevent fluctuations being generated in the country itself." (p. 265).

"That any country should dream of abandoning the existing international standard of value on such grounds sounds impossible," I wrote—but not so impossible now. In the same context, the book looks forward to "a new conventional international standard in place of gold." What I missed in these speculations was the idea, adopted in the Genoa Resolutions, that the co-operation of central banks could be used to stabilise the purchasing power of gold itself.

RALPH HAWTREY

July, 1961

CONTENTS

xi

CONTENTS

GOOD AND BAD TRADE

I

INTRODUCTORY

IN the last hundred years we have learnt to produce
wealth on a great scale. Our command of the necessaries, comforts, and luxuries of life, so far as the material
conditions of production are concerned, seems almost
boundless. But in the same period we have become
acutely aware of certain imperfections in the distribution of all this wealth.

The general principle by which the distribution is at
present governed is that those only are entitled to
share in the accruing wealth of society who assist in the
production of that wealth, whether through their
personal services or by permitting the use of land or
capital which is in their control. Whether this principle
would, if it worked smoothly, be a good or a bad one
is a question with which I do not intend to deal here.
The principle does, in fact, work imperfectly. For many
people who possess no accumulated property find themselves from time to time without the opportunity of
assisting through their personal services in the production of wealth, even though they would be perfectly
competent to do so if the opportunity offered. No one

can live without a share of wealth, and the community is faced with the alternatives of either supporting these people on some other principle than that of payment for services rendered, or letting them want.

The purpose of the principle of payment for services rendered is to put pressure upon all competent members of the community to work (except, of course, those who possess accumulated property). But if a man cannot find the opportunity to work, the pressure is useless ; and at the same time his faculties are being wasted so long as he remains idle. There are many contributory causes of unemployment ; unforeseen changes in the demand for a commodity, or in the places or methods of production ; imperfections in the organisation of industry, in the communication between would-be employers and would-be employed, in the training and selection of recruits for the skilled trades; jealousy and antagonism between skilled and unskilled labourers, between skilled labourers of different trades, between different branches of the same trade. But whatever the relative importance of these causes may be there is one dominating all-pervading fact which appears to require separate consideration, and the special import-ance of which has been admitted by most of the econo-mists and politicians who have studied the subject. Trade as a whole is subject to a well-marked though not quite regular wave motion, with a period from crest to crest or from trough to trough, which varies from four or five to about ten years. In the trough of the wave business is subject to a kind of paralysis. It becomes abnormally difficult to sell goods, and manufacturers find themselves compelled to reduce their output and consequently to turn adrift some of their workmen. At such times all the various causes of unemployment appear to be working with more severity than usual. On the other hand, on the crest of the wave, everything seems to prosper. Business is profitable ; manufacturers are overwhelmed with orders ; practically every competent workman can get work. These fluctuations of trade are important on many grounds, but it is on account of their bearing upon the unemployed problem that an explanation of their causes and true character is most urgently called for.

My present purpose is to examine certain elements in the modern economic organisation of the world, which appear to be intimately connected with the fluctuations. I shall not attempt to work back from a precise statistical analysis of the fluctuations which the world has experienced to the causes of all the phenomena disclosed by such analysis. But I shall endeavour to show what the effects of certain assumed economic causes would be, and it will, I think, be found that these calculated effects correspond very closely with the observed features of the fluctuations.

The general result up to which I hope to work is that the fluctuations are due to disturbances in the available stock of " money "—the term " money " being taken to cover every species of purchasing power available for immediate use, both legal tender money and credit money, whether in the form of coin, notes, or deposits at banks. The banking and currency systems of the world are so intricate and various, and apparently small differences acquire so much importance as the subject develops, that it will be necessary to begin with abstract and artificially simplified assumptions, and to take into account one by one those complexities which will be necessary to complete a true picture of the actual economic world.

The special importance of money in the theory of trade fluctuations is to be attributed to the fact that *all* branches of commerce and industry are equally dependent, and dependent in the same way, upon the use of money. Whether the economic influences connected with the use of money are great or small they will at any rate be far-reaching.

The principle of distributing wealth in return for services rendered or property lent is carried into effect through the instrumentality of money. The workman receives his pay, the capitalist his profits or interest, the landowner his rent, in the form of money. The money when received represents a power of purchasing commodities within the limit imposed by the amount received as compared with the prices at which the commodities are offered for sale. The producers of commodities depend, for their profits and for the means of paying wages and other expenses, upon the money which they receive for the finished commodities. They supply in response to a demand, but only to an effective demand. A want becomes an effective demand when the person who experiences the want possesses (and can spare) the purchasing power necessary to meet the price of the thing which will satisfy it. A man may want a hat, but if he has no money he cannot buy it, and his want does not contribute to the effective demand for hats. Or he may have money enough to buy a hat and yet may spend it on boots or other more pressing needs.

Economists often think it necessary to emphasise the fact that money is not wealth, but is a mere token of wealth, used to facilitate exchange. This is true, and must no doubt be grasped by every one who wishes to study economic questions. But at one time economists were so anxious to guard themselves from the fallacy of identifying money and wealth that they slipped into an almost pedantic disregard of the influence of money in economic phenomena. Although money is not wealth it is a most potent factor in economic organisation. And this is indeed so well recognised nowadays that it is hardly necessary to enter a warning against the prejudice which would condemn as superficial any theory claiming primary importance for purely monetary influences.

II

THE RELATIONS BETWEEN MONEY, PRICES, AND INCOMES

THE total effective demand for all finished commodities[1] in any community is simply the aggregate of all money incomes. The same aggregate represents also the total cost of production of all finished commodities. Supply and demand are not mere quantities, but are quantities produced or demanded *per unit of time*. Money income is money received per unit of time—it is so much a year, a month, a week, or a day. The supply of coal, or corn, is so many tons or quarters produced per unit of time—say in a year. The cost of producing all commodities at the rate per annum at which they are being produced is the cost of paying the persons who are assisting to produce them at the rate per annum at which they are being paid.

In England, of course, we have a gold currency. Debts above 40s. can only be legally discharged by the payment of gold or by the payment of notes, cheques, etc., convertible on demand into gold. But in some countries the currency is made up of notes which are themselves legal tender and which are not convertible on demand into gold. As a matter of fact, the countries

---

[1] Including consumable commodities, direct services, and fixed capital. This statement (like several others which follow) must be taken as true in principle, but subject to many qualifications which are not here relevant and the enumeration of which would be tedious.

6

which use an inconvertible paper currency are usually poor, backward, or politically unstable. But there is no reason why an inconvertible paper currency should not be successfully administered in an enlightened and advanced community without any undesirable consequences. For purposes of illustration it is often more convenient to deal with a country using inconvertible paper than one using a gold or other metallic currency, because the amount of currency in circulation is there wholly within human control instead of being dependent on the supply of a natural product.

Suppose, then, an imaginary community with an inconvertible paper currency. The total effective demand for all commodities per unit of time is the aggregate of all money incomes. The total cost of production of all commodities per unit of time is the aggregate of all money incomes. In order that the effective demand and the cost of production of all commodities per unit of time may be equated to a sum of money accruing per unit of time, the commodities must be priced in money, and the payments to the people engaged in production must be computed in money. The relative prices of the various commodities will be determined by the demand and supply of each. The *relative* remuneration of those who contribute their services or their property to assist in the production of wealth will be determined by the demand for the several forms of wealth produced and the supply of the several forms of services and property offered for that purpose. If every commodity sold in the unit of time is set down at its money value, the total will be the effective demand for all commodities. If every income is set down at its money value the total will be the cost of production of the same commodities. These totals are, as we have seen, equal, being merely the total money income of the community seen under two aspects.

But given that such and such commodities are being produced and consumed per unit of time, how will their respective prices and how will their total money value compare with the total stock of money in the hands of the community at any given time? Will a stock of legal tender currency equal to a week's income be sufficient? Or a month's income? Or a year's income? The paper money which we have assumed to be employed has no intrinsic value. Its value is due solely to the fact that the law decrees it to be legal tender, and therefore to be the legal evidence of the possession of purchasing power.

If the paper money is issued in denominations of dollars and cents, then income and prices will be calculated in dollars and cents. The general level of prices and incomes will in some way be proportional to the number of dollars in circulation. If by a stroke of a magic wand every note had its face value doubled, and at the same time every income, every price, every liability were also doubled, the business of the country could proceed precisely as before.[1] The only difference would be one of nomenclature. That amount of value which was called a dollar, would now be called two dollars, but *relative* prices and *relative* incomes would be unchanged. It is certain that, given the number of dollars or other units of currency in existence in any community, the number of such units per annum contained in the aggregate of money incomes is not a mere

---

[1] The degree of subdivision of the unit of currency for the purposes of small change is a mere matter of convenience, and is not relevant here.

matter of caprice. Since the aggregate of money incomes is proportional to the stock of money, it must be possible to establish some determining relation between them. How, then, is this relation to be revealed ? If a community whose aggregate money income amounts to an average of £40 per annum per head of population requires a stock of legal tender money equal to an average of £4 per head, there must be some reason why a stock of £20 a head is not required, and why a stock of £1 is not enough. There must be some reason why with £4 a head the income comes to £40, not £400 or £4 per annum per head.

It might be supposed that in a country using a metal coinage the answer was to be found in the cost of production of the metal. But this throws no light on the case of inconvertible paper.

It is necessary, in fact, to investigate a little more closely the manner in which the money in circulation is used. Assume, at first, for the sake of simplicity, that all transactions are carried out in ready money and that there is no banking system. It is perhaps natural to say that the money in circulation is used by being paid in exchange for commodities or services, and that the scale of incomes and prices depends upon the average number of such transactions for which each coin or note is used in the unit of time. That is, no doubt, quite true, but it does not give us much help, for we still have to discover what it is that determines for how many transactions a coin or note is used on an average in the unit of time.

In fact, the question was, *how* is the money used ? and the answer, that it is used by being paid in exchange for services or commodities, was only half an answer. The payment of a note[1] is only a momentary transaction. However often that may occur in a day, the note spends the greater part of its life reposing in some one's pocket or purse, or in some one's till or cash-box or strong-room. At any chosen moment, say 10.30 a.m. on the 13th March, 1913, practically all the money in the country will be reposing in pockets, tills, cashboxes, safes, or similar receptacles. A note here and there will be on its passage through the post or across a counter or from hand to hand, but the number at any single moment of time will be negligible.

The real question is, then, what determines the amount of money that a man will keep in his pocket, his till, his cashbox, or his safe ?

If his income is fixed, it will probably be paid at regular intervals : once a quarter, once a month, or once a week. At the beginning of each such interval he will find himself in possession of a sum which must last till the end of the interval. From this sum he spends portions from time to time to satisfy his daily needs. His expenditure will perhaps be less regular than his income, and so he will find it prudent always to have a moderate sum in hand to provide against unforeseen contingencies. He will endeavour, therefore, so to manage his affairs that, immediately before his next instalment of income becomes due, he will still have some money in his pocket. The precise amount which he will think it necessary to have will depend upon the character of the contingencies which he may be called upon to meet. Of course, no one would set to work to reckon out what those contingencies are, but every one

---

[1] It must be remembered that we are supposing only paper money to be used.

has some practical experience of unexpected disbursements, and one who has gained such practical experience will feel uneasy whenever his money in hand falls
below the prudent minimum. And besides unforeseen
contingencies he must provide against liabilities
(periodic or other) which are foreseen, but which are so
heavy that they can only be met out of the savings of a
considerable period. A man with weekly wages will on
an average keep less in his pocket than a man with a
monthly or quarterly salary. A man who pays a weekly
rent will keep less than one who pays a quarterly rent.
A man whose casual expenses are small will keep less
than one whose casual expenses are great. A further
complication will be introduced where earnings are
irregular, but it is unnecessary to discuss at length all
the possible variations of circumstances.

Thus every man has to keep a greater or less reserve
of money, or " working balance," which represents the
margin, up to date, of his income over expenditure.
This margin must be great enough to prevent his expenditure ever actually overtaking his income. If it is
up to this minimum, then, as income and expenditure
do not exactly keep pace, it will swell immediately after
large receipts or immediately before large disbursements
to a substantial sum.

If a steady excess of income over expenditure is
realised the reserve of money will grow. It may be
worth while to let it grow for a time, but a reserve
swollen beyond the amount necessary for a working
balance is a useless expense. Now and then, when the
reserve has passed this limit, the surplus can be invested.
If securities already in existence are purchased, the
money passes into the hands of the seller. To him it is

probably also an unnecessary surplus of ready money
to be promptly invested in other securities. As the retention of such a surplus involves the sacrifice of the
income that might be gained by investing it, the money
will, after circulating for a longer or a shorter time,
come to rest either in the hands of a man who needs to
replenish his reserve of ready money in order to bring
it up to the prudent minimum, or in the hands of a man
who invests it in a *new* enterprise. The process of investment in a new enterprise is quite distinct from the
purchase of existing securities. The new enterprise
must be started by the purchase of new capital, and the
money is expended in paying the cost of production
of this new capital. The capital may of course take an
infinite variety of forms : ships, factories, houses,
advertisements, fences, vehicles, roads, harbours, railways, machinery of all kinds and for all purposes, are
only a selection of such forms. But whatever form it
takes its cost of production will be made up, like the
cost of production of any other goods, of the incomes,
or contributions towards the incomes, of the persons
whose time or whose property is used in the process.
In fact, investment is merely expenditure, like all other
expenditure, except that the product is something that
can be expected to produce income continuously for an
appreciable period of time. Thus the money spent in
investment passes into the pockets of individuals and
helps to make up their working balances or their savings,
just like the money spent in producing more ephemeral
commodities.

The foregoing description relates to the position of a
man *quâ* consumer and investor, but his position *quâ*
producer is not in essence different. Production re-

quires to be financed in exactly the same way as house-
hold expenses. There must be a working balance of
money sufficient to bridge the greatest gap which
exists at any time during the process between the expenses and receipts up to date. A manufacturer who
undertakes to supply goods to a wholesale dealer will
have to spend considerable sums before he can deliver
the goods and receive payment. He must first buy his
raw material, and he must then pay wages to his workmen and rent for his factory during the process of
manufacture. Finally he gets in exchange for the
finished product a sum of money which should normally
be equal to all he has spent *plus* a margin or profit, and
he is then in a position to begin all over again, and undertake another wholesale order. In the same way the
wholesale dealer must be in a position to pay the manufacturer for the goods, and the cost of transport and
storage must be paid. The goods will gradually be un-
loaded upon the retail dealers, who will normally pay to
the wholesale dealer a sum sufficient to cover his payment to the manufacturer and all other charges. The
retail dealers in turn will recoup themselves with the
money paid by their customers who purchase the goods.
In fact, all the expenses of all the processes of production, transport, and sale are incurred in anticipation of
these payments by the consumers. And as the goods
are necessarily sold in driblets to the consumers, while
many of the preceding processes can only be carried out
economically on a large scale, it follows that large
working balances are necessary to finance both industry
and commerce.

We have now traced the situation of all the money
in a community in which there is no banking system.

The money is kept in pockets, tills, cashboxes, or safes, as a working balance to provide against the uneven progress of income and expenditure. In the case of a person who is saving, this reserve is periodically growing unnecessarily great, and he therefore periodically skims off the surplus and invests it. Money invested is really spent on the creation of capital, and this surplus is thus dissipated among his neighbours in the form of salaries, wages, interest, and rent, and is merged in their working balances. The aggregate of the working balances at any moment depends on the incomes and expenditures of the persons to whom they belong, and on the manner in which these incomes and expenditures accrue. Given the manner in which they accrue, the aggregate of the balances depends on the aggregate of the incomes and the aggregate of the expenditures. But the incomes and expenditures are simply the same quantity appearing on different sides of the account. And the aggregate of the working balances is simply the total stock of legal tender currency in the country. Here, then, in outline is the required relation between the total circulation and the total income of the country. The link connecting the two is to be found in the reserves of working balances of ready money which all recipients of incomes are impelled by prudence to maintain.

Money is merely purchasing power. This is especially obvious when the money used is paper only, without intrinsic value, and is not convertible as of right into anything of intrinsic value. The distribution of incomes among the people is the distribution of purchasing power, regarded as a continuing right, while the distribution of ready money among their pockets is the distribution of the accrued purchasing power not yet exercised. With an inconvertible paper currency which is sufficiently subdivisible, it cannot matter in terms of what units it is expressed. With given industrial and commercial conditions the relative proportions of incomes and the relative proportions of cash balances will be determined, whether the unit in which they are calculated is called a pound, a dollar, or a franc. Precisely the same reasoning applies to a metallic currency (such as that of India) the value of which is kept at an artificially high level by limiting the quantity coined. And it applies equally well to a freely coined metallic currency which circulates at the market value of the metal of which it is made. The only real difference in the latter case is that the supply of coinage depends on the supply of metal, either newly mined or diverted from other uses, whereas the supply of inconvertible paper or a restricted metal coinage is within the control of the Government.

Thus the case of a community using a freely coined metal currency does not require any separate consideration at this stage.

III

But it is time now to adapt these principles to the case of a community with a banking system. A bank may be defined as an institution which accepts a liability to furnish money *on demand*.[1] Other borrowers accept a liability to pay money on such and such a specified date, which may be near or remote. But a man who has deposited money with a bank has the right to resume possession of it at any time. This right he can at any time assign to any one to whom he wishes to pay money, either by handing him a bank-note or by drawing a cheque, according to the form the bank's liability takes. An assignable right to receive money on demand from a solvent bank is for practical purposes as good as money itself. It is indeed a substitute for the regular legal tender money and is called " Credit Money." In the country with no banks, which has just been considered, it is obvious that any rich man whose income and expenditure accrued in a specially irregular manner would be compelled to keep inconveniently high working balances. Still more would this be the case with large employers of labour and persons through whose hands large sums must pass in order to produce a relatively

---

[1] No doubt some institutions not technically "banks" accept such a liability, but they have many of the attributes of banks, and the definition given above is, at any rate, broadly if not universally true.

moderate net profit. For these and others in the same predicament a banker offers great advantages. He will relieve them of the necessity of providing a safe place for their money and of paying servants to watch it perhaps night and day. If the money entrusted to him exceeds a very moderate sum he will require no further remuneration for this service than the use of the money so long as it remains in his hands. He will pay interest on sums deposited with him if the depositor undertakes to give notice before withdrawing them, and he will be prepared to lend money in an emergency to any one of whose credit he is satisfied and who has reasonable security to offer. The result is that the man with a banking account need carry very little actual ready money in his pocket, or his cashbox, for he can meet the emergencies for which appreciable sums are required by drawing cheques; and his working balance (of which his balance in the bank thus forms the greater part) does not have to be so great as it would be if he could not count on being able to borrow. Thus his working balance consists not of a single reserve of ready money, but of a whole series of reserves like the successive reserves of an army. He can pay £1 out of the money in his pocket. To pay a sum of £10 he may have to draw a cheque. If he wants to spend £100 he will perhaps withdraw money on deposit. If he wants to raise £1000 he may mobilise his credit and anticipate his future receipts by borrowing from his banker.

Thus the aggregate of accrued purchasing power is no longer limited to the aggregate of the circulating medium. It is now made up of all the actual cash (and bank-notes) in people's pockets, tills, and cashboxes, *plus* all the amounts standing to the credit of their banking accounts. If the bankers simply kept all the money entrusted to them in chests, this total would be the same as the aggregate of the circulating medium.

But, of course, the bankers make their profits by lending out their customers' money. From the point of view of the banker this money is subject to much the same conditions as if it were his own property. That is to say, a certain portion must be set aside as a working balance, and the remainder, like the savings of the private person, can be invested or put out to interest. As in the case of the private person, the working balance is determined by the extent and nature of the liabilities which it will be called upon to meet. For small transactions it is more convenient to use money than cheques. Every one, therefore, carries about some ready money with him. The man who is earning weekly wages and paying a weekly rent probably has no banking account on which he can draw cheques. His employer must therefore obtain cash every week in order to pay him. This cash finds its way in the course of the week into the hands of shopkeepers, rent-collectors, omnibus companies, etc., who in turn pay it into their banking accounts. The well-to-do people, who receive their incomes at longer intervals and pay the rent by the quarter, usually have banking accounts, but they must, of course, cash cheques from time to time to meet their petty disbursements. Thus the banker's working balance must be sufficient to supply those of his customers who are employers of labour with enough cash to pay their weekly wages bills, and to supply all customers alike with their petty cash. The money spent in wages comes back very quickly to some bank or other through the shops, etc. For the moment it is not necessary to consider the manner in which the mutual liabilities of two banks will be extinguished. It may be assumed that practically all the money which is paid out of a bank on Saturday for the payment of wages will be paid back by the following Saturday. The payment of relatively large salaries may be assumed to be by cheque, so that no cash reserve need be held for that purpose. But the bank's well-to-do customers will periodically draw out an abnormal amount of ready money for occasions, such as holidays, which demand an unusual amount of petty expenditure and which affect a large number of people simultaneously. The banker must therefore hold in his till (1) the cash required by his customers to pay one instalment of wages to their employees, (2) the cash required to supply his customers with ready money both at normal times and at holiday times ; to these we may add (3) a moderate margin for contingencies. Now all these together represent a very small proportion of the banker's liabilities. A contractor will probably receive payment by cheque in large instalments at intervals of several months. The cheques as received will be paid into his banking account. He will pay his expenses, such as the cost of plant, raw materials, rent, etc., at appreciable intervals. One week's wages bill will be quite a small fraction of the sum standing at any time to his credit.

The shopkeepers again (though they, like others, will require money for their wages bills) will accumulate their takings at the bank over appreciable periods until they are required to pay wholesale dealers' bills or rent, or dividends. In fact, if the whole annual wages bill of the United Kingdom is £1,000,000,000 (a liberal

estimate) the weekly bill is under £20,000,000, a mere
trifle compared with the aggregate of deposits, etc., in
the banks, which do not fall far short of £1,000,000,000.

The reserve which a banker is positively obliged to
keep in normal times is thus a very small percentage
of his total liabilities—5 per cent is a liberal estimate.
But it occasionally happens that there is an abnormal
demand for money, that is, for actual tangible cash,
not for a mere balance at a bank. For example, in the
actual financial organisation of the world gold may be
needed to be exported to a foreign country to which
the conditions of trade have made the export profitable.
In a country which uses paper or silver as its circulating
medium, and in which no banker is therefore under an
obligation to honour his customers' cheques in anything but paper or silver, such a contingency cannot
arise. But in practice gold is the ordinary medium
(whenever any such medium is required) for the ultimate settlement of international debts, and this is so
because the great commercial countries of the world
have adopted gold as the material of their ordinary
internal legal tender currency. In those countries the
obligation of supplying gold for use in international
trade falls absolutely on the bankers. To be ready to
meet this and other similar obligations a banker is
bound to maintain a further reserve in addition to the
working balance kept for the purposes enumerated
above. Now this contingency may happen equally to
any bank. Any customer may wish to draw out large
sums of gold at a time when the market is asking for
gold. If every bank had to provide separately against
such an eventuality it would have to keep a very considerable portion of its assets in the form of a gold

reserve. But just as the individual can insure against contingencies by calling in aid his credit with his bankers, so the banker can insure against contingencies by calling in aid his credit with other bankers. He can lend or invest all but a moderate proportion of the money entrusted to him, and if he is suddenly called upon to pay out more gold than his reserve will meet, he can supplement it by borrowing from the other banks. Thus, instead of each bank having to be prepared to meet the maximum demand for gold that could fall upon it, it is only necessary for all the banks together to have enough gold between them (over and above their working balances) to meet the maximum demand that could fall upon the market as a whole.

But even this is not the ultimate refinement in the organisation of the reserve of money. Where each of a score of big banks depends upon all the others, there may in an emergency be a hitch at any point of the complicated chain of credit. If doubt is thrown on the solvency of any one of them, its position remains impaired unless it can persuade each of the others that its resources are adequate and realisable. Any one of the banks may at any time arbitrarily refuse to lend. There is no security that the aggregate of the reserves kept will be sufficient for all emergencies. In short, a community of banks with mutually dependent credit and mutually independent management will be weak from the absence of any central control. The solution which has been found by those of the great modern states which have been most successful in banking, is to set up one responsible central bank, more or less intimately associated with the Government. The other banks, instead of depending on one another, depend on the central bank. They are no longer responsible for keeping enough gold between them to supply the market in an emergency ; they merely maintain their working balances, and instead of keeping a further reserve in gold they open accounts with the central bank. Any bank which needs to find a large sum in gold can draw upon its account with the central bank, and, if the balance to its credit is insufficient, can borrow. Every demand for gold, outside the current transactions of every day, then falls upon the central bank, and the directors of the central bank are at all times in immediate touch with all such demands. They are the first to receive the gold imported into the country ; they supply gold when it is needed for export. It is for them to calculate, having regard to all possible emergencies, how much gold they must hold in reserve. How they are to solve this problem, and what steps they must take to put their conclusions into practice, are questions which will have to be dealt with at a later stage.

We are now in a position to give in outline a complete answer to the question, what is all the money in the country doing ? It is maintaining working balances : *first*, the working balances of all the members of the community so far as their daily expenditure of actual cash is .concerned ; *secondly*, the working balances of all trading concerns which pay or receive cash across the counter ; *thirdly*, the working balances of the banks ; *fourthly*, the cash reserves of the central bank. This aggregate of cash supports a far larger aggregate of purchasing power, in the form of rights possessed by people with banking accounts or by holders of banknotes to obtain cash on demand. Behind this, again, comes the power (though not an absolute right) to borrow on good security up to an imperfectly defined limit. The aggregate of purchasing power and the aggregate of borrowing power are, *other things being equal*, proportional to the aggregate of cash.

We shall have to consider the relations between these aggregates when other things are not equal in more detail at a later stage. It is sufficient here to point out that the aggregate of money incomes bears the same relation in a community with a banking system to the aggregate of purchasing power, including credit money, as in a community without a banking system to the aggregate of legal tender currency.

IV

HITHERTO we have been dealing with the relations between the stock of money in circulation and the various economic entities such as incomes, prices, cost of production, etc., into which the unit of currency enters. But it is necessary also to turn for a moment to the conditions of production, so far as those conditions concern our present purpose.

Production is normally undertaken with a view to profit. It is intended that the thing produced shall be something which people want, and which they want keenly enough to buy at a price which will cover the cost of production. The prospect of receiving such a price is intended in our form of society to be the producer's sole motive to produce. Producers who produce for other motives are philanthropists—a term of reproach. And at any rate it is, in general, true that producers produce for profit.

What then is the " cost of production " ? This cost falls into two categories, the wages of labour and the fees (such as rent or interest) payable to the owners of property used in the process.

The remuneration of the ordinary undistinguished labourer is simply the sum which the employer must pay him for giving up his time. However much or however little actual toil the labourer is called upon to

24

do, his working day is an opportunity for assisting in the production of wealth, and so long as his time is occupied to the exclusion of other remunerative pursuits, he must be paid according to the standard prevailing in the labour market. Under the competitive conditions of the market this standard prescribes at any time a more or less definite rate of remuneration for independent adult labour. In trades which require special aptitudes the wages will rise perceptibly above the standard, the extent of the difference depending largely on the ease with which the necessary aptitudes can be acquired. But practically all trades demand some skill, and the man who acquires no skill has little chance of maintaining the position of an independent citizen at all. So, although, for this and many other reasons, wages do vary from trade to trade, it is right as a first approximation to say that, outside the relatively few who are paid high salaries for using their judgment and initiative, a week's wages represents the market value of the services of an able-bodied man for a week, and this standard wage is the fundamental unit in reckoning cost of production.

Of the more highly paid employees who do not conform to this description, the only function which it is necessary to consider is that of supervising and directing the wage-earners. A number of men cannot combine to perform one task unless they are under some unified control. The people responsible for exercising this control must issue directions to the workmen so that each may know every day what he is to do. They must also decide how many men are to be employed and what plant will be necessary. All these functions may be either ill or well carried out. If they are ill carried out the consequence will be the retention of some men who are given nothing or not enough to do, or who are given work to do which does not need to be done or will have to be undone. This is waste. Waste usually consists in occupying the time of a competent workman without applying it to any useful purpose. The employment of competent supervisors will reduce waste. The ability of one man may by this channel come to be worth the wages of 1000. If such ability is very rare he may receive a salary approximating to the sum which he saves. If it is fairly common, his salary will be quite moderate. If practically any one is competent, without special training or ability, to undertake the business, the remuneration will ultimately sink to the ordinary market wage.

Thus, so far as labour is concerned, the basis of the cost of production is the number of days' work for which a market wage must be paid, *plus* the cost of supervision.

The other element in the cost of production is the fee paid to the owner of property used in the process. This property falls into two classes, land and capital.

" Land " means the earth's crust. But, for economic purposes, it is necessary to distinguish two different ways in which land is employed to assist in the production of wealth. First, the actual stuff of the earth's crust is used to provide the raw material of industry, either inorganic materials obtained from mines, quarries, etc., or organic materials grown in the soil. Secondly, the processes of manufacture and transport, and, indeed, all the activities of mankind demand *space*. Any given piece of the earth's crust may be wanted for the production of materials, such as crops or minerals, or it may be wanted merely to afford space for buildings, roads, etc. Where there is a private ownership of land, and free competition, each plot will in general be put to the use which its owner expects to be most profitable.

A plot of land may be hired for a fee representing the market value of the most profitable use to which it can be put, and proportional to the period for which it is hired. If the most profitable use is the production of materials, the fee paid will depend partly upon the natural efficiency of the land in producing those materials, that is to say, the fertility of the soil or the richness of the mines or quarries ; but it will depend partly also on the convenience of the situation in relation to the agencies of manufacture and transport and to possible consumers. If, on the other hand, the most profitable use is for the erection of buildings, the value of the land will depend almost entirely on its situation and conformation ; it will, in fact, be almost exclusively its value as space, or " site value."

It is not necessary here to enter into all the intricacies of the theory of economic rent. The foregoing summary will be sufficient to distinguish land from capital, to which we now pass.

Capital may, for our present purpose, be defined as those material aids to production which are created by human agency. The characteristic of capital so defined is that it derives its value in exchange from its use in producing other things which have an exchangeable value. In a sense, no commodity has value in itself, but only as the means to the satisfaction of some need. If I want a loaf, it is as the means to the satisfaction of my hunger. But if I want an oven to bake my loaf, the oven is merely the means of obtaining the loaf. The loaf, as a direct means to my satisfaction, is classed as a consumable commodity; the oven, as a means to the production of a consumable commodity, is capital.

Capital, like other exchangeable commodities, has its cost of production. The cost of production of capital is in turn an element in the cost of production of the commodities which the capital is used to make. If the capital takes the form of raw material or anything else which is used up in a single process, the whole of its cost of production must be included in the cost of production of the finished product. But the case of fixed capital which is used again and again, perhaps continuously for many years before it is used up, requires further consideration. It is still true that this fixed capital derives its value exclusively from its use as an aid to production. By its means more commodities can be produced for less labour ; it is, in fact, a labour-saving device. But this saving is effected at the cost of the labour expended in producing the fixed capital. How is this labour to be divided in the form of cost of production among all the commodities produced ? And how great a saving in the cost of production of these commodities will justify a given expenditure of labour in producing the capital ? It is clear, at any rate, that the saving must be greater than the expenditure. If the two were merely equal, there would be no inducement to produce the capital and to wait for years to complete a return which after all would be no more than could have been obtained without any waiting at all. Some margin of the saving of labour over the cost of the capital is necessary to pay the capitalist for the delay in obtaining consumable commodities in exchange for his expenditure. The greater the delay the greater must this margin be.

A man who is working with his own capital may not distinguish in his accounts the precise saving which he realises by any extension of his capital which is paid for from his own resources. But a man who extends his capital by means of borrowed money must pay a fee, in the form of interest, for the sum borrowed, and he can only decide whether this is or is not worth while, by calculating whether the annual saving due to the extension of capital will or will not cover the annual payment of interest.

A capitalist who borrows will borrow with a view to adding to his business that one of all possible extensions of capital which seems likely to produce the greatest annual additional profit in proportion to its first cost ; and this proportion will represent the highest rate of interest at which he will be willing to borrow. An intending lender will lend to that capitalist who offers him the highest rate of interest. This, of course, is the ordinary operation of supply and demand in an open market. The effect is to equalise the rates of interest asked and offered so that there is a single market rate (differences due to differences in the credit of the borrowers may for the present purpose be neglected). This state of affairs can only be reached if every business is supplied with capital up to such a point that an extension of its capital would earn additional profit equal to or less than the interest upon the cost of the extension. If an extension in any business would earn a greater profit than this, lenders will tend to select that business for their operations, until it also is supplied with capital up to the prevailing level. It is hardly necessary to say that the speculative element in these operations makes the practice very different indeed from the theory. But still, there remains this central fact that people engaged in industry can afford to borrow money for the purchase of new capital at a rate of interest not greater than the probable annual saving of labour due to the new capital as compared with its cost. It is important to notice that the primary function of capital (once the absolutely necessary minimum is provided) is to save *labour*. We are accustomed to express this by saying that it saves or earns *money*, but the saving of labour is the ultimate physical fact. If mechanical road sweepers save the rates, that is because one man with a mechanical sweeper can do the work of several with brooms. The reduction in the number of men is a physical fact, of which the reduction in the cost is merely an economic consequence. In any country in which the amount of capital per head increases, the rate of interest has a tendency to fall. If one generation has discovered all the most profitable openings for the investment of a fund of capital amounting to £100 per head, and if the next generation finds openings for the investment of a fund of capital amounting to £150 a head, the new openings must, other things being equal, be less profitable than the old. On the other hand, new inventions and improvements in organisation have a precisely contrary tendency. Every new invention is, in fact, a new opening for investment, and until the invention has come into the most extended use for which it is adapted, this investment may command profits far exceeding the market rate of interest. But in practice neither of these tendencies can, at any rate in a wealthy modern state, act very quickly. The additions made in one year to the national stock of capital are small compared with the total; the progress of invention may be rapid now and then in one particular industry, but it is rarely widespread enough to have any very marked or sudden effect on trade as a whole.

Here then is the answer to the question, how does capital enter into the cost of production? It appears in the form of the interest on the cost of production of the capital. This is in appearance a vicious circle, for capital enters into the cost of production of capital. But that objection does not really arise, for the capital already in existence and the new capital in process of creation are in competition with one another. The cost of production of the old capital becomes, for practical purposes, the cost at which new capital like it might be produced, and the rate of interest tends to be that which, assumed on new and old capital alike, will just make the employment of new capital profitable.

The foregoing remarks apply to *fixed* capital, that is to say plant, more or less permanent in character, which will continue so long as it is kept in repair to earn in labour saving a certain percentage on its first cost. But the term capital includes commodities, such as fuel and raw materials, which are consumed in a single process of production, but which still are only *means* of production. An interval, short or long, elapses between the production of such commodities and the completion of the consumable goods into the manufacture of which they enter. This interval, like delay arising from any other cause in the fruition of the products of labour, must be paid for. From the point of view of the capitalist who controls the means of production, there

is no important difference between the application of
labour and plant to one purpose or another, and he will
exact payment for this delay on the same terms as for
the longer delay arising in the case of fixed capital.
In other words, circulating capital and fixed capital will
be in competition as fields for investment, and the same
rate of interest will be required from both. Thus in any
business working under normal conditions the price
received for the finished product should be sufficient to
cover not merely rent and interest on fixed capital and
the actual expenditure on labour and materials, but
interest at the market rate on this expenditure for the
period which has elapsed since it was incurred.

Up to this point we might regard the cost of production, including rent, interest on capital and payments for supervision, as well as wages, as expressed in
terms of days' work. The finished product represents
the work of so many men for so many full days, and the
other charges represent fees in respect of various savings
of full days' work, due to the favourable situation of the
land occupied, to the skill of the supervising staff, and
to the use of mechanical appliances.

But in the market the cost of production is expressible
in money. The condition of profitable production is
that the price obtained for the finished commodity shall
not be less than the cost of production. Both price
and cost must be measured in money. In order to
determine on what scale they will be measured, it is now
necessary to return to the machinery of distribution
already described.

It was laid down that the total effective demand
for all commodities is simply the aggregate of all
incomes, and that the same aggregate represents the

total cost of production of all commodities. Some qualification requires to be made in this broad statement. Incomes are made up partly of earnings, partly of rent and interest. The greater part of these are directly connected with the production of commodities. Some, however, such as the earnings of actors, musicians, lawyers, and doctors, and of people engaged in one way or another in the work of government, are the remuneration of services which do not contribute to the production of any concrete commodities. These services, by an artificial stretch of language, may themselves be classed as " commodities."

But a further correction is still required. The definition of capital as the material aids to production excludes a number of forms of property, such as houses, gardens, and furniture, which are consumable commodities, but in which, as being of a durable character, savings are ordinarily invested, and for the use of which an annual sum comparable to interest may be paid. The amount of such annual sums will be brought by competition into line with the rate of interest. The income derived from this kind of property can only be regarded as part of the cost of production of a commodity if the enjoyment of the property for a specified time, not the possession of the property itself, is taken to be the " commodity." It is perhaps unnecessarily pedantic to strain language by such devices, but the exceptions thereby surmounted have not enough importance to merit separate treatment at the cost of sacrificing not only symmetry, but also clearness.

We can now say simply that the aggregate of incomes is equal to the total cost of production of all commodities. Each income represents the purchasing power per annum of its possessor. This purchasing power is exercised in part upon consumable commodities, in part upon capital. In so far as it is exercised upon capital it is none the less expended in the purchase of commodities, but these commodities are *durable*, whether they are used for immediate enjoyment, or as the means to the production of other commodities. Thus the whole income (except such as goes to increase the working balance) is *spent*, whether it is saved (i.e. invested), or not. In the long run all incomes are being completely expended, and the aggregate of all incomes over a period of time is the aggregate of all people's expenditure over the same period, and is therefore equal to the aggregate of the sums paid for all articles bought for consumption or investment, or in other words to the aggregate of the sums received for all articles, perishable or durable, sold for those purposes.

If we can imagine a perfectly stable condition of society in which the birth-rate and death-rate are equal ; in which the aggregate income, the stock of money, the aggregate of bank balances, the scale of prices, are all constant ; in which all tastes, all demands, all processes remain unchanged ; in which capital is always sufficiently renewed and replaced, but never extended ; in such a condition of society the standard wage represents a definite and constant sum of money per week, which forms the basis of the cost of production of all commodities. The prices of commodities will be permanently equal to their respective costs of production (inclusive, of course, of all monopoly and scarcity profits, which may be assumed to exist and to be permanent). This is simply to imagine society without those fluctuations of trade which form our present subject, and to which we are now prepared to turn.

In dealing with fluctuations it is necessary to qualify in one important respect the equations which have been established above. Those equations relate the aggregate of all incomes, the aggregate cost of production of all commodities produced per unit of time, and the aggregate of all purchases (or sales), for consumption or investment, per unit of time. Each of these terms, however, is not an actual quantity of money existing at a moment of time, but a rate at which money is accruing. These rates must all in the long run be equal. But the process of production, culminating in sales, and the process of receiving an income, culminating in purchases, both occupy time. During the period occupied by the manufacture of a commodity the national income, of which its cost of production is part, may increase and diminish once and again. It still remains true that all the actual rates of income at a particular moment, if added together, make the total cost at which all the commodities that are in course of production at that moment are being produced. But the cost at which a commodity " is being produced " may change while it is still in course of production. In the same way at a particular moment all commodities may be deemed to have a definite price, but the price may vary from day to day.

From the reasoning in this chapter it can be seen in what sense incomes, prices, and the cost of production of commodities, are merely the machinery of distribution. An income is a claim to receive so much money per unit of time, and money, even if it be composed of gold reckoned at its bullion value, is *quâ* money merely that medium in which the State has decreed that debts may legally be discharged. The really essential facts about the economic condition of a country are that such and such commodities are being produced at the cost of so much labour and skill, and by means of so much capital ; and that these commodities are being .consumed in such and such proportions by the members of the community. The only use of the elaborate system of money and credit is to provide the necessary legal evidence of purchasing power in the hands of those who possess that power. It is because money plays this subordinate part that the quantity of money in circulation is not relevant (in any important way) to a consideration of total national wealth. This is especially obvious in the case in which all money is inconvertible paper, but it is really just as true where gold is used ; for where gold is used, the nation (except for the convenience of having a stock of international money permanently available for adjustments in foreign trade) can only benefit directly from its gold by replacing it by some other medium of exchange such as paper money, that is to say, by ceasing to use the gold as money, and using it in some other way.

But the fact that money is merely machinery does not prevent it from having profound and far-reaching effects on the production and consumption of wealth. Though the quantity of money in circulation is not relevant to a consideration of total wealth, *changes* in the quantity of money in circulation react upon the industrial and commercial state of the country, and have effects of the greatest importance.

V

A MONETARY DISTURBANCE IN AN ISOLATED COMMUNITY
WITH NO BANKING SYSTEM

THE first step in the examination of trade fluctuations
will be to consider what will happen if the theoretical
equilibrium of incomes, expenditures, money, etc., is
disturbed. Let the equilibrium exist, as in the perfectly
stable society described above, and let it be disturbed.
First, suppose the disturbance to take the form of a
sudden diminution of the stock of money. We may
assume that only paper money is used, and that there
is no banking system. The cause of the diminution is
not here relevant, but it might be effected by the
Government withdrawing, in the form of taxes, more
money than usual, and permanently withholding the
surplus from circulation. The effects would then be
spread evenly over the whole population.

Now a certain proportion of incomes are fixed in
amount and more or less permanent. Whatever may
happen to increase or diminish the national stock of
money, there is no immediate reason for the recipient of
a fixed income to alter the " working balance " of money
which he retains in his pocket or his cashbox. But the
majority of incomes are either variable or at any rate
precarious. The profits of manufacture, of transport,
and of retail trade are variable. The wages and salaries
of the majority of employees, though less variable, are
precarious.

Before the withdrawal of money from circulation, every member of the community may be assumed to have adjusted his working balance of money in hand so as to fit the income he was accustomed to receive and the expenditure he was accustomed to incur. After the withdrawal, therefore, some at any rate of the members of the community, having had to pay more taxes than usual, will find that they are in danger of a shortage. In the absence (as assumed) of a banking system, it will be necessary for them to restrict expenditure for a time in order to replenish their balances.

But though any one may replenish his balance by economising, it is clear that no transfers of money from one individual to another can replenish *all* the balances, the total of which has been definitely reduced by a certain amount. A new equilibrium can only be found by a change in incomes which will make a reduced scale of balances sufficient. The next step, therefore, is to consider the effect upon variable and precarious incomes.

The restriction of expenditure by some members of the community represents a corresponding restriction of the receipts of others. Those who are engaged in the production of a particular commodity, including the labourers and their supervisors, and the capitalists and landowners who participate (so far as they participate) in the production of the necessary raw materials, in the intervening processes of manufactures up to the completion of the article, in the process of transport from the several places of manufacture to the several places at which the finished goods are offered for sale, and finally in the various services included under the head of retailing, such as advertisement, storage, selection in accordance with the customer's directions, delivery at the customer's house, etc. etc., all these people depend for the remuneration of their services ultimately on the money paid by the consumer. The goods have no value, except such as is purely speculative, until they are actually in the consumer's hands. Any one engaged in one of the intermediate processes depends upon the people engaged in the immediately succeeding processes for his reward, and thus through a continuous chain all depend ultimately upon the money which is given to the retailer by the consumer, who is the only person whose function is not " intermediate."

The whole boot trade, including the labour, land, and capital engaged not only in manufacturing boots, but in breeding the beasts to produce the leather, and in transporting and retailing the finished boots, is dependent in the last resort for its wages, rent, and interest upon the money expended by members of the community in buying boots for their own use. The aggregate of wages, rent, and interest paid to the boot trade per diem will tend to be equal to the daily expenditure on boots, and cannot in the long run diverge from that daily expenditure.

A contraction of the money in circulation entails, as we have seen, a restriction of expenditure by members of the community. This restriction of expenditure may be assumed to extend impartially (but not necessarily equally) over the whole area of consumable commodities. For the moment (before any palpable signs of this change have appeared) each trade will be in the position of continuing its output at the old rate and incurring daily liabilities for wages, rent, and interest which can only be met if that output is disposed of at

the old price. The first symptom of changed conditions
will be diminished sales by the retailers, involving a
diminution in their working balances.

As less commodities are sold, the retailers will order
less from the wholesale dealers, who in turn will order
less from the producers. If the producers do not receive
sufficient orders to employ their capital and labour at
full time, they must either reduce their output, or reduce
their prices, or both.

In the perfectly stable community price is permanently equal to cost of production, and the producers'
choice when the price falls is therefore between reduction of output and reduction of cost of production.
Cost of production is ultimately the cost of paying the
incomes of the persons engaged in production, including,
besides the wages of labour, the salaries of the supervising and directing staff, the interest of the capitalist,
and the rent of the landlord.   Of these several elements
in cost of production some, such as rent, or the interest
on money borrowed on the security of the business, will
be fixed charges ; others, such as the wages bill and the
profits of the owner or of the shareholders, as the case
may be, will be variable. The fixed charges cannot be
reduced unless the business actually becomes insolvent,
all other expedients having proved ineffective.

The first encroachment, when sales fall off, will of
course be made upon profits. A business which has been
paying high dividends can afford to continue its full
output at a certain reduction of price without suffering
actual loss. But in some cases this will not be sufficient.
Those businesses which have not a sufficient margin of
profit must reduce either the number or the pay of
their employees. In so far as the adjustment is made

by the dismissal of hands the total output of the community will be diminished.

This process could, theoretically, be pushed so far that the proportional decrease in the number employed and in the national output would be equal to the proportional decrease in the money in circulation. In that case the old scale of incomes and prices could be maintained ; but the incomes with the appropriate balances of money would be shared among a portion only of the community, upon whom would be thrown in some form or other the burden of supporting the unemployed (unless the unemployed were deported, left to starve, or otherwise disposed of).

On the other hand, if the adjustment could be made entirely by a suitable diminution of wages and salaries, accompanied by a corresponding diminution of prices, the commercial community could be placed forthwith in a new position of equilibrium, in which the output would continue unchanged, and distribution would only be modified by the apportionment of a somewhat larger share of the national product to the possessors of interest, rent, and other kinds of fixed incomes. In fact, the change in the circulating medium is merely a change in the machinery of distribution, and a change, moreover, which, once made, does not impair the effectiveness of that machinery. If the habits of the community are adapted without delay to the change, the production of wealth will continue unabated. If customary wages and customary prices resist the change, the adjustment, which is bound to come sooner or later, will only be forced upon the people by the pressure of distress.

The symptom of incomplete adjustment is the diminu-

tion of employment, either a dismissal of superfluous
hands or a reduction of hours. For this there is (apart
from a restoration of the national stock of money to its
old level) no remedy but the reduction of money wages
to the point which will enable producers to resume their
former activities and dispose of the output without
incurring a loss. This reduction of money wages does
not involve a proportional reduction of real wages, for
it is accompanied by an all-round reduction of prices.
But there will, in general, be some slight reduction
of real wages, representing the change in the balance of
wealth as between the holders of fixed incomes and other
members of the community.

The time taken in reaching the new position of
equilibrium will probably depend on the willingness of
employees to accept the reduced wages. It will, perhaps, be hardly evident enough to them that the accept-
ance of reduced wages will provide a cure for their loss
of employment, but the mere presence of a body of unemployed ready to accept work on almost any terms
would have a tendency to depress wages. Whether the
process is long or short, the result is very much what
theory would lead us to expect, a general fall in the
nominal value of everything which is measured in
money.

The above description deals merely with the consequences of a single abrupt change in the quantity of
money in circulation, a change to which society can
ultimately adapt itself in a renewed equilibrium. If
the changes are gradual and continuous the community
may be in a permanent condition of fluctuation without
ever reaching economic equilibrium at all. If for a
period the stock of money continuously diminishes,

precisely the same causes will be at work as in the period following a sudden diminution. Wages will cling to their customary rate until the stress of unemployment begins to drive them down; they will follow the downward movement of money and prices at an interval; and at last, when the movement of prices stops, there will be an accumulated weight of unemployment only to be relieved by a continuance of the movement of wages. We are not for the moment concerned with the possible *causes* of changes, continuous or otherwise, in the stock of money; but a reversal of the previous movement might take place, in the form of a gradual increase in the stock of money and in the scale of prices, before wages have fallen to the equilibrium point, and might swallow up the unemployed in a new era of increasing trade before the equilibrium point is ever reached.

So far we have considered the effect of a contraction of the currency principally on the wage-earner. Incidentally, however, we have touched upon capital.

The capitalist, as we have seen, earns interest by providing labour-saving appliances. According to economic theory he selects for his operations that opening which will enable him to save the greatest amount of labour per annum with a given initial expenditure, i.e. to earn the greatest rate of interest. At any moment there will be a particular marginal or market rate of interest such that all enterprises promising a higher yield have already been seized upon, and it has not yet been worth while to undertake any enterprise whose promised yield is lower. In the perfectly stable community, capital is renewed and replaced but never extended. There will in any year be a constant amount of new investment replacing an equal amount of industrial failure, and the rate of interest will be constant. If the monetary equilibrium in such a country is disturbed, the movement will end, as already described, after a greater or less interval of time, in a state of equilibrium on a new scale of incomes and prices, but with the whole system of production and distribution very nearly unchanged.

In this new condition of equilibrium the market rate of interest, depending as it does upon the physical qualities of the various labour-saving contrivances in use, will presumably be the same as before the change. But in the interval of adaptation the rate of interest will be modified.

For[1] consider any project for investment at a time when there is a general tendency for the prices of commodities to fall. If the rate of interest under stable conditions is 4 per cent, then any new equipment of fixed capital which cost £10,000 would, so long as the stable conditions continue, save labour to the value of £400 per annum. But if the prices of commodities are falling at the rate of 2 per cent per annum, then after one year the fixed capital will be worth only £9800, and the labour saved will be worth only £392 per annum. Suppose that the fall of prices is expected to continue for two years so that the total fall is expected to be 4 per cent. Then a man who invests £10,000 in this way will expect to receive £392 a year hence, and in the second and every subsequent year £384 3s. 2d.[2] He will, in

---

[1] The theory indicated in the following paragraphs has been clearly and fully explained by Prof. Irving Fisher in his book *The Rate of Interest*.

[2] i.e. *£392 less* 2 per cent.

fact, get very little over £384 a year by way of interest
on his £10,000. If, therefore, he wished to lend the
£10,000 to some one else, instead of himself expending
it on the provision of fixed capital, 4 per cent would be
too high a rate of interest for the borrower to offer him.
Competition always tends to make the rate of interest
prevailing in the market equal to the actual yield
expected from the use of money in business. This under
the conditions assumed has fallen to £3 17s. per cent, or
thereabouts, and a security yielding a fixed £4 in
perpetuity would be worth nearly £104.

The foregoing applies to permanent investment.
Business, however, involves a certain amount of temporary borrowing. A sum of money is borrowed for a
specified period of a few months, weeks, or even days,
at the end of which it is repaid. The rate of interest
charged in such a transaction calculated at a rate per
cent per annum would, under stable conditions, be
exactly equal to the rate of interest for permanent
investments. But when the prices of commodities are
falling this ceases to be the case. If the rate of interest
under stable conditions is 4 per cent and prices are
falling at the rate of 2 per cent, then a man who borrows
£100 for six months and pays interest at 4 per cent will
be a loser. For not only will he pay £2 by way of interest
(4 per cent for half a year), but he will have to repay the
capital of £100, though the goods bought with it will
have sunk in value to only £99. In fact, the transaction will have cost him £3, or 6 per cent per annum on
his capital. To redress this the rate of interest offered
for loans must fall to 2 per cent per annum. Accordingly the effect of the falling prices of commodities is far
greater on the rate of interest for temporary loans than

on that for permanent investments. Indeed, the rate of interest on permanent investments would not drop to 2 per cent unless the fall of prices by 2 per cent per annum were expected to continue in perpetuity. The fall is expected to outlast the period of a short loan, and so the rate of interest for that period is diminished by the whole 2 per cent. The fixed capital purchased may be regarded as yielding 2 per cent per annum for the first two years, during which there is a loss through depreciation of the market value of the plant to set against the gross yield, and 4 per cent thereafter. Thus in one sense the permanent and temporary investments still yield the same rate per cent, but the rate on the former is variable and will rise to its old level some time after the period of the latter has expired.

Of course this is all a matter of abstract theory. Borrowers and lenders do not take the future purchasing power of money into consideration when they settle the rate of interest. But any useful examination of the practical bearings of this theory must be postponed to the next chapter, when the inclusion of a banking system in our hypotheses will bring our investigations into closer approximation to reality.

It may be objected that even in theory, on the assumptions made, the ordinary profits of business have already been greatly diminished or even wiped out by the loss of purchasing power and failure of demand. No doubt this is so, so far as the profits yielded by existing fixed capital are concerned. And it is also true that there will be little or no investment in new enterprises for increasing the output of commodities. The existing equipment of capital is insufficiently employed in meeting the diminished demand, and there is no use in adding to it until the demand for commodities has revived. Under the stable conditions assumed capital is renewed and replaced, but never extended. This need not mean that there are no new enterprises at all, but that the new enterprises will only just be sufficient to replace the failures. When the contraction of the currency occurs and profits vanish, the starting of new enterprises will be interrupted and the total quantity of capital in use will diminish. But this does not mean that the provision of new capital in industry ceases altogether. For capital is primarily a means of saving labour, and so long as labour is employed at all, labour-saving contrivances will fulfil their function, whether they are used to increase output or to diminish the wages bill.

Thus low profits are associated with flagging demand in two quite distinct ways. On the one hand, the profits on existing capital are encroached upon through wages resisting the fall which the failure of demand requires. On the other, the profits on any new investment in which the *money* value of the original capital is to be maintained unimpaired are diminished. It is by the profits on *new* investments that the market rate of interest is governed. Once fixed capital has been created it can be used for no other purpose than that for which it was designed, and its sole value lies in its future yield. But while it is only projected, it may still be abandoned and the labour necessary for its creation can be applied to some other purpose. So long as this is possible the action of the investor will be guided by a comparison of the first cost with the future yield, and it is from that comparison that he arrives at a rate of interest. A transaction in which the first cost is no longer a factor will not directly affect the rate of interest. A man may pay a capital sum for a business ready equipped with capital, but the rate of interest assumed for the purpose of the transaction will really be based on the possible yield obtainable from alternative investments. Indeed, probably the seller intends to lay out the purchase price in one of these alternative investments. According to theory, then, the prevailing rate of interest should be the rate which existed before the disturbance, as modified by the falling prices of commodities.

To complete the survey of the consequences of a contraction of the currency it is necessary to refer to the question of how much money will be available for investment. In other words, what will be the effect on saving ? At the beginning there is a general depletion of cash balances. It must be remembered that the savings applied to investment are usually surpluses periodically taken out of growing cash balances. These surpluses will for the moment be less than they would otherwise have been. In the case of a person with a fixed income the rate at which the cash balance grows will be the same as before the contraction, and he will soon begin to accumulate savings at his usual rate. A person with a variable income will find his income permanently diminished, and he will take time to adapt his habits to his changed circumstances. If he thought it worth while to save before, however, he will probably think it worth while to save still. As prices fall and profits are restored he will again find himself in a position to accumulate a surplus on his cash balance. But in the interval his savings will have been continued at a much diminished rate, if not altogether suspended, or he may even have drawn upon his accumulated wealth to meet his trade losses.

Employees will fall into two classes, those who remain in employment and who, as retail prices fall more quickly than wages and salaries, may even find that their cash balances grow more quickly than before, and those who, falling out of employment for a longer or a shorter time, are compelled to draw upon past savings or to run into debt. The net result is that savings are perceptibly less than in normal times.

The effects of a sudden expansion of the circulating medium may be investigated in precisely the same manner as those of a sudden contraction. People find themselves one day with more money in hand than they expected. Each proceeds to spend his surplus, some using it to meet wants and desires which must otherwise have remained unsatisfied, others investing it or using it to increase their stock of permanent property. In any case the money is applied to the purchase of commodities or services, and the surplus is merely transferred from the buyer to the seller. So long as the scale of incomes remains unchanged, commercial equilibrium is disturbed ; whoever possesses a share of the surplus proceeds at once to get rid of it. Thus the number of purchases per day is above the normal. The stocks of the retailers begin to be depleted. The retailers give increased orders to the producers, who in turn take what measures they can to increase their output. If economic conditions have hitherto been stable, and if the rate of wages has been in harmony with market conditions, there will be no large reserve of unemployed labour to draw upon for this purpose. But there will presumably be efficient men temporarily unemployed between one job and the next, and inefficient men chronically underemployed, besides veterans who are too old to continue in work, and youths who are hardly old enough to begin. There will thus in any case be a reserve of a sort, which can be drawn upon by any employer who is willing to take special pains to seek for it, or who can afford to pay wages for labour which is not fully effective. The sudden acceleration of purchases will make it worth an employer's while to take these steps. It will also be possible for him, at any rate as a temporary expedient, to set his men to work overtime. But on the assumptions we have made, excluding as they do the case where a period of expansion immediately succeeds a period of contraction and inherits therefrom a burden of unemployment, the possible extension of the productive capacity of the community would not be very great. The retailers being unable to obtain the execution of their orders for new goods without a considerable and increasing delay, could only protect their stocks from depletion by raising retail prices, and at the same time they would be prepared to pay increased wholesale prices to the producers. When the rise of retail prices has so far checked the increase in demand that the producers can meet it, a state of temporary equilibrium will have been reached. Incomes, so far as they are variable, will have been increased by the increased profits of business, and the corresponding increase in cash balances will have used up the expanded currency. But there is, so far, nothing in all this process to affect the remuneration of labour, except the employment of the few additional hands who are obtainable.

In the normal condition of a stable society, a certain number of businesses would always be failing, and new businesses would be filling their places. At a period of expansion, however, many, if not all, of the businesses which would otherwise be failing are enabled to earn some profits and to keep their heads above water.

The new businesses will not find the usual supply of hands cast adrift by the failures, and they will have to compete with the existing businesses to provide themselves with labour. Here is an influence tending to increase the rate of wages. So long as money wages remain at their old level, whoever has the privilege of employing labour receives an abnormal rate of profit, above the actual value of his own services and the labour-saving virtues of his capital and land. While this continues he is in the position of getting something for nothing out of his employees, and it will be to the interest of his rivals in business to entice away his men by offering them a little more. As a matter of fact, it is not always possible to induce a workman to leave his employment merely by offering him a higher wage, and therefore it may take a considerable time for this influence in the direction of higher wages to take effect. But the influence exists, and, until it is worked out, economic equilibrium will not be restored.

It is necessary to consider what, in the meanwhile, is happening to the profits of capital. The increase in the amount of money in hand causes, as has been seen, an increase in the amount of money spent on commodities in a given period of time, and in particular causes an increase in the amount spent on the provision of capital or, in other words, invested.

But an increase in the amount of money to be spent in investment does not necessarily of itself affect the rate of interest. The amount annually invested in any community represents a very modest proportion indeed of the total capital already existing, and the effect of one year's investments, be they great or small, in depressing the rate of interest is very slight. The rate of interest will measure the actual return which may reasonably be anticipated from the most favourable investments still remaining open; the investors, however much money they may wish to invest, need not accept less ; however little, cannot exact more.

Now, as just explained, to any one engaged in business the interval between the first inflation of the currency and the final adaptation of the rate of wages is exceptionally profitable. The income account for that period will value the receipts at the enhanced prices then prevailing, while among the disbursements, though the cost of materials will have risen, the cost of labour will be initially low and will only rise gradually.

But this extra profit accrues to the owner of a business not in his capacity as a capitalist, but in his capacity as an employer of labour. It is a consequence of the willingness of his men to continue working at a wage which, through the fall in the value of money, has become less than the economic price of their labour. Probably it is not open to a man who is starting a new enterprise to get this extra profit, or at any rate to get the whole of it ; for he will find difficulties in obtaining a supply of labour, all the regular workmen being already employed in the existing enterprises.

But though the abnormal profits due to the prices of commodities outstripping that of labour will have but little effect on new investments, the market rate of interest for short loans will be subject to influences similar in kind and contrary in effect to those which lower the rate during a period of depression.

A man who has borrowed, say, £10,000 for the purpose

of increasing or improving the plant of his business will
find, when the time comes for repaying that amount,
that the additional plant which he has set up is worth
more than £10,000. Suppose, for instance, that the
money is borrowed for six months during which prices
appreciate 1 per cent, and that, if prices were steady,
he would have found it worth while to borrow at 4 per
cent per annum, or £200 for the six months. Then in
consequence of the rise of prices his plant will be worth
£10,100 at the end of the six months and he will have
obtained profits in addition sufficient to meet the half-
year's interest of £200. He can therefore afford to pay
£300 on account of interest, or 6 per cent per annum.

And here, as before, the effect on the rate of interest
for permanent investments is relatively small. If the
rate of interest is expected to be raised for two years to
come from a normal rate of 4 to 6 per cent by the force
of rising prices, a perpetual annuity of £4 will be worth
only about £96, representing a yield of about £4 3s.
per cent.

The outcome of this chapter is that we have followed
out to its consequences an arbitrary discontinuous
change in the quantity of money in an economic organisation which has been assumed to be in certain ways
arbitrarily simplified. The consequences revealed correspond remarkably with the well-known characteristics
of actual trade fluctuations. On the one hand, a contraction of the currency has been shown to occasion
the slackening of demand for all classes of commodities,
the fall of prices, the lack of employment, the shrinkage
of profits, and the low rate of interest which are the
concomitants of a trade depression. On the other hand,
an increase of the currency has been shown to lead to a

stimulation of demand, a rise of prices, a high demand for labour, inflated profits, and a high rate of interest, all of which are the symptoms of active trade. Our assumptions are too narrow and artificial, however, for us to draw any useful conclusions as yet, and in the next chapter we shall take a further step towards giving reality to the argument.

VI

A MONETARY DISTURBANCE IN AN ISOLATED
COMMUNITY WITH A BANKING SYSTEM

HITHERTO we have considered the problem of fluctuations in a highly abstract and artificial community—one in which there are no banks and no foreign trade. In order to bring the theory adopted into line with actual conditions it is necessary to examine the effect of these two complications in modifying our conclusions.

It will be convenient, first, to deal with the banking system, and for the present still to ignore all international influences. The part played by a banking system in relation to the working balances of money held by the individual members of the community has been briefly explained above. The bank has received various sums from its depositors and is permanently under the obligation of repaying those sums on demand. That obligation may be represented either by a banknote for the sum deposited, or by an account between the depositor and the bank, conferring upon the depositor the right of drawing cheques, or, in other words, of instructing the bank to pay money either to himself or to some third person.

For the present we will assume, for the sake of simplicity, that the banker's obligations are represented by deposits and not by notes. To be in a position to discharge its liabilities the bank need not retain in the form of legal tender currency all the money which it has received. Provided a portion is retained sufficient to meet all reasonably probable demands for cash, the remainder can be either invested, or as is more usually done, lent for a moderate and definite period, which may be a few days or several months. We are not here considering the sudden creation of a banking system in a country where there has hitherto been none, and we need not therefore imagine a banker tying up judicious proportions of his gold in a bag and setting out to look for a borrower. We may assume a complete banking system in full working order, with a nicely adjusted system of reserves, based on long and carefully sifted experience. In such a banking system there is no necessary connexion between the total of the deposits and the amount of coin which has been paid to the banks. A banker may at any time grant a customer a loan by simply adding to the balance standing to the customer's credit in the books of the bank. No cash passes, but the customer acquires the right, during the currency of the loan, to draw cheques on the bank up to the amount lent. When the period of the loan expires, if the customer has a large enough balance to his credit, the loan can be repaid without any cash being employed, the amount of the loan being simply deducted from the balance. So long as the loan is outstanding it represents a clear addition to the available stock of " money," in the sense of purchasing power. It is " money " in this sense which will play, in a community possessing banks, the same part as money in the stricter sense of legal tender currency would play in the fictitious bankless community whose commercial conditions we have previously been considering. This is the most distinctive feature of the banking system, that between the stock of legal tender currency and the trading community there is interposed an intermediary, the banker, who can, if he wishes, create money out of nothing. We have now to find out how this functionary uses his power and under what limitations he works. Something has already been said of the contingencies for which he must provide. Whenever he grants a loan and thereby creates money, he must expect a certain portion of this money to be applied, sooner or later, to purposes for which legal tender currency is necessary. Sums will be drawn out from time to time to be spent either in wages or in small purchases, and the currency so applied will take a little time to find its way back to the banks. Large purchases will be paid for by cheque, involving a mere transfer of credit from one banking account to another, but the recipient of the cheque may wish to apply it to the payment of wages, etc. Thus the principal limitation upon the banker's freedom to create money is that he must have a reserve to meet the fresh demands for cash to which the creation of new money may lead.

He will as a rule, at any time, have in hand a sufficient balance of legal tender currency to support his outstanding liabilities. If his customers diminish this balance by drawing out more cash than they pay in, he will find himself with less than a sufficient balance, and he will endeavour to diminish correspondingly his outstanding liabilities ; that is to say, he will be more reluctant to grant new loans or to renew existing loans when they fall due. If, on the other hand, his cash balance increases, he will be in a position to increase his loans correspondingly.

In trade a seller encourages or discourages buyers by lowering or raising his prices. So a banker encourages or discourages borrowers by lowering or raising the rate of interest. If he raises the rate of interest, some intending borrowers will find the profits which they expect to realise from using the borrowed money insufficient to pay the interest, and it will no longer be profitable to them to borrow. If he lowers the rate of interest, some enterprises which would have involved a net loss or an insufficient profit at the old rate will become profitable.

It is clear that the interdependence of the rate of interest and the total amount of credit money in existence necessitates a complete reconsideration of the effects of a change in the stock of legal tender money. For simplicity we will set out as before by studying the effects of the arbitrary withdrawal from circulation of a portion of the currency, and we will suppose this to occur in a community the commercial and industrial conditions of which have hitherto been absolutely stable. The currency may be assumed, as before, to be inconvertible paper or token coinage, so that there is no free and automatic supply of fresh currency to be drawn upon when a portion is withdrawn.

The first effect of the contraction of the currency is that the working balance of cash in the hands of individual members of the community will be diminished. The precise proportion in which this diminution is shared between bankers and other people does not matter, for those who have banking accounts will quickly draw out enough cash to restore their working balances. As soon as this process is completed we have two effects ; first, that the greater part, indeed practically the whole, of the currency withdrawn comes out of the banks' reserves, and secondly, that the total amount of purchasing power in the community (i.e. currency in circulation *plus* bank balances) is diminished by the amount of currency withdrawn. One consequence of the existence of a banking system is that a given diminution in the stock of currency produces at this stage much less than a proportional diminution in the total of purchasing power. For example, if the total of purchasing power be £1,000,000,000 and the total of currency in circulation and in reserve £250,000,000, a 10 per cent reduction of the currency will initially involve only a $2\frac{1}{2}$ per cent reduction in purchasing power; the currency will become £225,000,000 and the purchasing power £975,000,000. If this could continue as a permanent condition, the extent of the trade depression and all other fluctuations would be very much diminished, but, of course, this result is only attained by a depletion of the banks' reserves below the level demanded by their liabilities. This the bankers cannot acquiesce in, and they will proceed to restore their reserves by discouraging borrowers, and in particular by raising the rates of interest which they charge for loans. In a stable community there will, of course, be a stable market rate of interest, but the mere diminution of purchasing power will of itself, in the manner previously explained, tend slightly to lower the market rate. For this is one of the concomitant effects of a trade depression, and the diminution of purchasing power, so far as it goes, will begin to produce a depression even before the supply of credit money has been affected. But until the bankers interfere, the depression is relatively small and probably works slowly. The bankers' action is the first important development. The bankers raise the rate of interest in order to restore their reserves. The actual effects of this step require to be considered in some detail. For this purpose a somewhat more detailed investigation of the manner in which business is financed is necessary.

The business of production is carried on from day to day, and the expenses accrue continuously. The business of retailing is likewise carried on from day to day, and the receipts accrue continuously. Between these two processes, however, there ordinarily intervene the stages of transportation, wholesale dealing, etc., in which the goods can only be economically dealt with in large quantities. As we have already seen, the financing of business consists primarily in providing the necessary working balances of money to enable these successive processes to be conveniently dovetailed together, and the greater portion of a banker's loans is composed of advances for this purpose. He advances money to the producer for the payment of wages in anticipation of the money which will be received from the wholesale dealer for the finished product, and which will enable the producer to repay all the advances in a single sum. He advances money to the retailer to buy a consignment of goods from the wholesale dealer, and receives repayment perhaps in instalments, more or less as the goods come to be disposed of to customers. The varying circumstances of different kinds of business give rise, of course, to corresponding varieties in their financial needs, but fundamentally the function of the banker as a lender is to enable his customers to avoid accumulating disproportionately large balances for some time before large disbursements or after large receipts.

The financial needs of any given business will be greater or less according as its output grows greater or less. If a man receives a larger order than usual he will have to make correspondingly larger payments for raw materials, wages, etc., in the interval before the goods are delivered, and will want to borrow proportionately more from his banker. Conversely, if he has less work on hand than usual he will ask less accommodation from his banker.

We are now supposing that the banker wishes to discourage borrowers, and for that purpose raises the rate of interest. It may be pointed out that, within limits, a banker can restrict loans directly by refusing to lend at all for the more speculative enterprises submitted to him, but in practice such action is hardly applicable except to new departures. If a customer established in business presses for a loan to carry on operations on the same scale as before, the banker would not ordinarily refuse. Thus, as against borrowers in legitimate business, the banker's weapon is the rate of interest. He will lend as readily as before to customers of good credit, but will make a higher charge for the money lent.

What precise effect will this rise in the rate of interest have on the borrowers ? The two principal classes of borrowers are the producers and the dealers. The producers will, of course, find the cost of production of commodities slightly increased. A manufacturer who receives an order from a wholesale dealer will quote a slightly higher price in order to cover this extra cost. If this rise in wholesale prices is reflected in retail prices there will be some slackening of demand, since the national purchasing power remains unchanged. But, in general, changes in the rate of interest such as we are considering are too small to affect retail prices immediately. The dealers would probably, in the first instance, pay the increased price to the producers without disturbing retail prices at all.

But the dealers themselves will be influenced by the rate of interest. One of the special functions of a dealer is to keep a stock or " working balance " of the goods in which he deals. This is necessary to enable him to meet the varied needs of his customers without delay. Now a dealer borrows money to buy goods, and repays the money as the goods are sold. Consequently when his stocks are large his indebtedness to his banker will be correspondingly large. The extent of the stocks which he sees fit to keep will be based on experience, but can, of course, be varied within fairly wide limits without much risk of inconvenience. When the rate of interest goes up he will be anxious to reduce his indebtedness, so far as he can, without incurring serious inconvenience. He can reduce his indebtedness if he can reduce his stocks of goods, and he can reduce his stocks of goods by merely delaying replenishment when they are sold. But the orders received by manufacturers come from the dealers who want to replenish their stocks. Consequently the manufacturers will at once find that they are receiving fewer and smaller orders. The money which the dealers would otherwise have been using to pay the manufacturers for goods, they are using to extinguish their indebtedness to their bankers. The effect, from the point of view of the manufacturer, is very nearly the same as that which was shown in the last chapter to ensue upon a contraction of the currency in a country without banks. That is to say, he experiences a slackening of demand, and in order to relieve the resulting restriction of output he lowers prices so far as the existing expenses of production will permit. This lowering of prices will enable the dealers to lower retail prices, a measure which would ordinarily stimulate demand. But in the meanwhile the reduction of stocks by the dealers and the restriction of output by the producers will have been accompanied by a diminution of the indebtedness of both producers and dealers to the banks, and this diminution of the bankers' assets will have been accompanied by a diminution in their liabilities, i.e. in the supply of credit money. The balances of money in the hands of the public are therefore decreasing, and the superstructure of incomes erected thereon is simultaneously shrinking.

The result is that as fast as the dealers reduce their stocks at one end by retarding the process of replenishment, they find that their stocks accumulate at the other end in consequence of a flagging of the demand from the consumer. Their stocks, therefore, are on the whole depleted little, if at all, but there is a continuous decline of both wholesale and retail prices of commodities, and this decline of prices, involving a fall in the money value of a given stock of goods, helps to maintain the decrease of indebtedness, and therefore of credit money.

And other tendencies will be contributing towards the same result. Any one who intends to undertake any industrial or commercial enterprise, involving, as such enterprises almost invariably do, the borrowing of money, will be inclined to postpone the commencement

of operations until money can be borrowed on more
favourable terms.   Extensions, renewals, or even
repairs of plant can be postponed for a few weeks or a
few months.   Company promoters will wait till money
is easier before they launch their ventures.   In fact,
every one will be unwilling to borrow at 6 per cent,
if he can wait without inconvenience till he can borrow
at 3.   And, of course, a high rate of interest imposed
for the express purpose of restoring the bankers'
reserves will necessarily be a temporary measure.
But all this means a curtailment of expenditure.   A
curtailment of one man's expenditure means a curtailment of another man's receipts, and so there arises a
still further restriction of output.   The process differs
from that described in the last chapter chiefly in being
more gradual.   The diminution in the stock of money,
instead of occurring suddenly, is caused progressively
by the action of the trading world under the influence
of the high rate of interest.   It should be observed,
however, that the slackening of the dealers' orders to
manufacturers is caused in the first instance not by the
diminution of purchasing power, but directly by the
high rate of interest, which discourages the accumulation of stocks.

   The high rate of interest will continue until the
bankers are satisfied that their liabilities in the form of
credit money (i.e. to pay cash on demand) are no longer
excessive in proportion to their reserves of cash.   When
this stage has been reached the rate of interest can be
reduced again.   But there is still much to be gone
through before the normal progress of business can be
resumed.   Throughout the period of high interest there
has been a progressive restriction of output and fall of

prices. The same pressure of distress that we found to operate in the case dealt with in the last chapter will have been at work. The working classes will have been under-employed and there will be a tendency towards the fall of wages. But this tendency will presumably not have had its full effect. Production, and therefore employment, will still be below the normal. In the succeeding stages, however, there will be no further reduction in the supply of money. The bankers have restored their reserves and are satisfied. The circumstances, therefore, resemble those which arise in the corresponding stages in a community without banks. The aggregate of purchasing power is on the reduced scale corresponding to the reduced stock of money; the productive resources of the community will not be fully employed until the level of prices is reduced in the same proportion; prices cannot be reduced until the cost of production is sufficiently reduced; and the cost of production can only be reduced as wages are reduced. Wages, therefore, are the key to the situation. The banks have only to see to it that their loans are kept at a constant level through the variations of output, of stocks, and of prices which will ensue. The demand for loans will not vary greatly, since output and prices will be moving in contrary directions. Practically the banks will only have to see to it that the rate of interest charged coincides as closely as may be with the earning power of money in business.

A new complication is introduced, however, into the theory of the rate of interest on short loans by the bankers' manipulations, and some further examination is necessary to make the subject clear.

In the absence of a banking system we found that two

distinct elements had to be taken into consideration in calculating the rate of interest. First, there was the rate which represented the actual labour-saving value of capital at the level of capitalisation reached by industry. This ratio of labour saved per annum to labour expended on first cost is a physical property of the capital actually in use, and under perfectly stable monetary conditions is equal to the market rate of interest. It may be conveniently termed the " natural rate." But, secondly, where monetary conditions are not stable, the market rate diverges from the natural rate according to the tendency of prices. When prices are rising the market rate is higher, and when falling lower, than the natural rate, and this divergence is due to the fact that the actual profits of business show under those conditions corresponding movements.

And now, thirdly, we find that where a banking system is in operation the market rate does not even coincide with this second rate of interest, which, as it represents the true profits of business prevailing for the time being, may be called the " profit rate." The market rate is in fact the bankers' rate, and is greater or less than the profit rate, according as the bankers wish to discourage or encourage borrowing. This theory is somewhat complicated, and we have yet to face the problem, postponed from the last chapter, of how far a theory into which so abstract a concept as the purchasing power of money enters can give a true account of the actions of practical men. We have just shown that it is the *dealers* in goods, rather than the producers, who are influenced by the bankers' manipulations of the rate of interest. And this is so because the dealers are holders of stocks of goods, the cost of holding which is directly and seriously affected by the rate of interest. But the cost of holding stocks of goods is affected just as directly and seriously by changes of price. If prices are falling a dealer will want to hasten his sales and delay his purchases ; if prices are rising he will want to delay his sales and hasten his purchases. In the former case he will decrease, in the latter he will increase his stocks. In the former so high a rate of interest will not be needed to induce him to curtail his borrowing as in the latter. In fact, if the cost of holding £10,000 worth of goods for six months is £200 it does not matter to the dealer whether this is made up of £100 interest at 2 per cent *plus* £100 on account of a fall of value from £10,000 to £9900, or whether it is made up of £300 interest at 6 per cent *less* £100 on account of a rise in value from £10,000 to £10,100. Consequently, for the banker's purposes, a "high" rate of interest is one which is above the profit rate, and a " low " rate of interest is one which is below the profit rate, and it is only when the rate of interest is equal to the profit rate that there is no tendency towards either an increase or decrease in temporary borrowing. In any of the three cases the rate of interest may be either above or below the natural rate. If the natural rate is 4 per cent and the profit rate in consequence of falling prices is only 2 per cent, a market rate of 3 per cent is " high," and will result in a curtailment of borrowing. If prices are rising and the profit rate is 6 per cent, a market rate of 5 per cent is " low," and will be compatible with an increased borrowing.

In the case we are now considering we assumed the disturbance to be a departure from perfectly stable conditions, in which the market rate of interest would be identical with the " natural " rate. On the contraction of the currency occurring the bankers raised the market rate above the natural rate. But at the same time the fall of prices began, and there must consequently be a fall of the profit rate below the natural rate. As we now see, the market rate may actually fall below the natural rate, and so long as it remains above the profit rate it will still be a " high " rate of interest.

When the restoration of the bank reserves is completed the market rate will drop down to equality with the profit rate, and they will remain equal to one another and below the natural rate until the fall of prices has gone far enough to re-establish equilibrium.

The restoration of the bank reserves is a process which calls for a little explanation. If, to return to the numerical illustration used above, the total stock of legal tender currency is £250,000,000 and the total of bankers' loans is £750,000,000, and if the former is reduced suddenly by 10 per cent, i.e. to £225,000,000, the total purchasing power in the community will at first be £975,000,000. If of the £250,000,000 £100,000,000 was required for general circulation and £150,000,000 for bank reserves, then, with a total purchasing power $2\frac{1}{2}$ per cent less, £97,500,000 will be required for general circulation, leaving a reserve of only £127,500,000 to support the bankers' loans of £750,000,000. The bankers must have £150,000,000 to justify that amount of loans ; or they would be content with £127,500,000 if their loans were reduced to £637,500,000.

They raise the rate of interest, with the result that the total amount of loans outstanding is gradually reduced.

But this process results in less money being required
for general circulation, so that the reserves at the same
time show signs of increasing. For example, by the time
the outstanding loans have been reduced to £700,000,000,
and the total purchasing power to £925,000,000, the
currency required for general circulation will be only
£92,500,000 and the reserves will have risen to
£132,500,000. Equilibrium will be finally restored
when the loans have reached £675,000,000, the circulation £90,000,000, and the reserves £135,000,000. Thus
the effect of the high rate of interest is both to reduce
the outstanding loans and to increase the reserve.[1]

The problem of an inflation of the currency is affected
by the existence of a banking system in somewhat the
same way as that of a contraction. The immediate
effect of an abrupt addition to the stock of money will
be to raise the bank reserves above their previous level
by, practically, the amount of money added. This, as
constituting an addition to the total amount of purchasing power, will start an acceleration of purchases
and an expansion of profits, but these phenomena will
be on a restricted scale so long as the amount of bankers'
loans (which constitute the greater part of the available
purchasing power) remains unchanged.

The bankers, however, are no more willing than other
people to keep larger stocks of cash than prudence
requires. They will therefore be readier than before
to grant loans, and will continue to be so until the

[1] In these figures it has been assumed for the purposes of illustration
that the cash in circulation necessarily bears a fixed proportion to the
aggregate of credit money. At a later stage we shall find that in
practice this is not the case, and that the failure of the cash in circulation to vary with the aggregate of credit money is of great importance
in the theory of fluctuations.

amount of outstanding loans has so increased that their
reserves are no longer unnecessarily great. The proper
procedure for this purpose would be to lower the rate
of interest. But the profits of trade have already been
stimulated, and the demand for loans at the old rate,
which represented the old profits, will therefore in any
case be greater. Even if the bankers continue to ask
the same rates for loans as before, the aggregate amount
of loans will grow steadily. Moreover, every day that
an addition is made to the aggregate amount of bankers'
loans, that addition is being made to the aggregate
amount of the community's purchasing power, and is
thus contributing to intensify the expansion of trade
and to raise the profit rate of interest. There is no
reason why the bankers should raise their rates up to
the profit rate until the outstanding loans have so far
expanded that the reserve of legal tender currency
remaining in their hands is no longer more than sufficient. One of the most important features of a period
of expansion, in contrast with one of contraction, is
that the action of every one concerned is much less
fettered in the former than in the latter. During a
depression bankers are driven to exact higher rates for
loans by the visible melting away of their reserves,
manufacturers are driven to sacrifice their profits and
turn their men adrift by a sheer inability to dispose of
their goods, workmen are driven by stress of unemployment to accept lower wages. But when trade is
expanding a banker can take advantage of the rising
rate of interest or of the more rapid extension of his
loans at the existing rate of interest as he chooses ; the
workman may not find out for a long time that the
market will, if pressed, yield him employment at higher

money wages ; and the trader is glad enough to sit still
and accept the high profits which fortune has given him.
In general, as the aggregate of bankers' loans gets
within sight of the limit set by the available reserve,
the bankers will begin to consider what steps they ought
to take to prevent that limit being passed, and they will
see to it that the rate of interest on loans is fixed at or
near the profit rate.

As in the case of a depression the adjustment of wages
may be fast or slow, but cannot in any case be completed until after the extension of the aggregate of
bankers' loans is completed. Until the adjustment of
wages is completed the profit rate of interest (and
therefore also the market rate) will be above the
natural rate.

Again, as in the case of a depression, the reserve will
not remain constant while the amount of bankers' loans
is being adjusted. If initially the amount of legal
tender currency is £250,000,000, of which £100,000,000
is in circulation and £150,000,000 in the bank reserves,
and the amount of bankers' loans is £750,000,000, and if
the amount of legal tender currency is abruptly increased
to £275,000,000, representing an increase of 10 per cent,
then the amount of purchasing power will at first be
increased from £1,000,000,000 to £1,025,000,000, an
increase of $2\frac{1}{2}$ per cent only. The amount required for
general circulation should increase in the same proportion to £102,500,000, leaving £172,500,000 as a
reserve to support loans to the amount of £750,000,000.
As the loans grow the amount of currency demanded for
general circulation will increase and the reserve will be
diminished. Thus, when the outstanding loans have
reached £800,000,000 the amount of purchasing power

will be £1,075,000,000 and the currency in circulation will be £107,500,000, so that the reserve will be only £167,500,000. Finally equilibrium will be reached when the loans are £825,000,000, the circulation £110,000,000, and the reserve £165,000,000.[1]

---

[1] See footnote on p. 69.

VII

ORIGINATION OF MONETARY DISTURBANCES IN AN ISOLATED COMMUNITY

In the last two chapters we have postulated a perfectly arbitrary change in the quantity of legal tender currency in circulation. However closely the consequences traced from such an arbitrary change may correspond with the phenomena we have set out to explain, we have accomplished nothing till we have shown that causes which will lead to those consequences actually occur. With the general problem of how trade fluctuations are generated we cannot cope satisfactorily till we have extended our field of inquiry to include an international system with the multifarious economic institutions which are to be found in the actual world.

At the present stage, however, it is already possible to make a preliminary survey of the causes of fluctuations with the advantage of an artificial simplification of the problem. And at the outset it must be recognised that arbitrary changes in the quantity of legal tender currency in circulation cannot be of much practical importance. Such changes rarely occur. All the great commercial countries of the world use gold currencies, and in a gold currency arbitrary changes cannot occur at all. Gradual changes in the supply of gold do occur, but, though they are of considerable importance in the theory of trade fluctuations, as will be shown in a subsequent chapter, they are not sudden enough to produce the effects elucidated in the preceding chapters.

But what we are looking for is the origination of changes not necessarily in the quantity of legal tender currency, but in the quantity of purchasing power, which is based on the quantity of credit money. A change in the quantity of credit money will serve our purpose even if it is not based on a corresponding change in the quantity of legal tender currency. For example, if the bankers suddenly came to the conclusion that the proportion of reserves to liabilities previously maintained was too low, and decided to increase it, this would necessitate a reduction in deposits exactly similar to the reduction which in the last chapter we supposed them to make in consequence of a reduction in the actual stock of legal tender currency. Or there might be casual variations in their reserves. These reserves simply consist of that portion of the existing supply of cash which happens for the moment not to be in the pockets, tills, cashboxes, etc., of the public. The amount of money which any individual carries about with him at any time is largely a matter of chance, and consequently there may very well be variations in the cash in circulation and therefore contrary variations in the reserves, which are really of the nature of casual fluctuations, or at any rate are not attributable to any cause which could come within the bankers' cognisance.

And here we must take note of two very important economic laws. First of all, when the bankers have thus disturbed the course of trade owing to their failure to diagnose correctly a casual increase in their reserves, the disturbance is always liable to be exaggerated in the following manner. We have already remarked that when the bankers are extending their loans, there is theoretically a simultaneous tendency towards a diminution of their reserves, for the increase in the aggregate of purchasing power demands a proportional increase in the currency in circulation. But in practice the increase in the circulation (and the decrease in the reserves) will probably lag behind the increase in purchasing power. The additional loans are placed by the bankers to the credit of the borrowers, who intend presumably to employ the money in their business. As soon as the money begins to be used, cash begins to be drawn out against this credit. But cash is required mainly for the payment of wages, and the increased profits of trade are not at first accompanied by a proportional increase of wages. The increase of the circulation at the expense of the reserves will therefore be a gradual process spread over the whole interval between the first extension of the bankers' loans and the final adjustment of wages. First, the improvement in employment, even before there is any increase of wages, will increase the total earnings of the working classes, and then, when wages have reached their limit, the cash in their hands will still go on accumulating for a time, before the process of investment, through savings banks or otherwise, becomes sufficiently rapid to use up their savings as they accrue. Unless the bankers are prepared for this development they will invariably find themselves bound, at the end of a period of active trade, to curtail their loans again. And in a case where they have been misled by a casual increase in their reserves into relaxing their terms for loans as if there were a permanent increase in the circulating

medium, the subsequent recovery will be complicated
by the same cause. The contrary principle is also true,
that when there is a contraction of trade profits fall
before wages, and the banks reduce credit money more
than is strictly necessary.

Secondly, it is important to observe that whenever
the prevailing rate of profit deviates from the rate of
interest charged on loans the discrepancy between them
at once tends to be enlarged. If trade is for the moment
stable and the market rate of interest is equal to the
profit rate, and if we suppose that by any cause the
profit rate is slightly increased, there will be an increased
demand for loans at the existing market rate. But this
increased demand for loans leads to an increase in the
aggregate amount of purchasing power, which in turn
still further increases the profit rate. This process will
continue with ever accelerated force until the bankers
intervene to save their reserves by raising the rate of
interest up to and above the now enhanced profit rate.
A parallel phenomenon occurs when the profit rate,
through some chance cause, drops below the market
rate ; the consequent curtailment of loans and so of
purchasing power leads at once to a greater and growing
fall in profits, until the bankers intervene by reducing
the rate of interest. It appears, therefore, that the
equilibrium which the bankers have to maintain in
fixing the rate of interest is essentially " unstable," in
the sense that if the rate of interest deviates from its
proper value by any amount, however small, the
deviation will tend to grow greater and greater until
steps are taken to correct it. This of itself shows that
the money market must be subject to fluctuations. A
flag in a steady breeze could theoretically remain in

equilibrium if it were spread out perfectly flat in the exact direction of the breeze. But it can be shown mathematically that that position is " unstable," that if the flag deviates from it to any extent, however small, it will tend to deviate further. Consequently the flag flaps.

The effect of these two principles in exaggerating any casual change in purchasing power is really the fundamental cause of fluctuations. Their operation will be dealt with more fully when we come to the general discussion of the origination of fluctuations in the world as it is, and we need not dwell further on them at present.

There are, however, other economic influences which at any rate affect even if they do not produce fluctuations. The state of trade, for example, is always held to be very intimately related with the state of credit. The tendency, indeed, is to exaggerate the importance of credit in the subject, but that it has considerable importance is not open to doubt. Credit money is composed of the obligations of bankers, and if a banker cannot meet his obligations the credit money dependent upon him is wholly or partly destroyed. Again, against his obligations the banker holds equivalent assets, together with a margin. These assets are composed chiefly of two items, legal tender currency and loans to traders. The solvency of the banker will depend largely on the reality of these assets, and the value of the loans will depend in turn on the solvency of the borrowers.

The most effective method of securing loans is by the instrumentality of bills. A dealer gives an order to a manufacturer for goods to the value of, say, £10,000, to be delivered in four months. The manufacturer will buy the necessary raw material and employ the necessary labour to produce the goods, and in order to do this he will wish to borrow a sum of money comparable to the £10,000 which he is to receive. He draws a bill for £10,000 payable four months hence on the dealer, and the dealer by "accepting" the bill pledges his credit that the money will be forthcoming. When both the parties to the transaction have vouched for it the manufacturer can take it to his banker and get the bill "discounted," that is to say, he will receive the money shown on the face of the bill, *less* interest up to the period when the bill falls due. The whole value of the manufacturer's efforts in producing the goods depends upon there being an effective demand for them when they are completed. It is only because the dealer anticipates that this effective demand for them will be forthcoming that he gives the manufacturer the order. The dealer, in fact, is taking the responsibility of saying how £10,000 worth of the productive capacity of the country shall be employed. The manufacturer, in accepting the order, and the banker in discounting the bill, are both endorsing the opinion of the dealer. The whole transaction is based ultimately on an expectation of a future demand, which must be more or less speculative. But the banker is doubly insured against the risk. Both the dealer and the manufacturer are men of substance. If the dealer cannot dispose of the goods for £10,000, he is prepared to bear the loss himself. He expects some of his ventures to fail, and others to bring him more than he counted on. Taking the rough with the smooth he will probably make a profit. Even if now and then he finds that

over a period of time he has suffered a loss, he probably
has sufficient property to enable him to meet the loss
without failing to meet his obligations to the manufacturer. And if the dealer becomes insolvent there is
still the manufacturer to save the banker from loss. A
manufacturer usually has a considerable quantity of
fixed capital which would enable him to borrow on
mortgage to meet such a liability. Where bills are not
used a banker may lend on the sole credit of a dealer
or manufacturer, relying on the value of the business
to which he lends as the ultimate security for the loan.

Now if a contraction of credit money occurs, the
consequent slackening of demand and fall in the prices
of commodities will lead to a widespread disappointment
of dealers' expectations. At such a time the weakest
dealers are likely to fail altogether. Moreover, the
credit of the manufacturers is also likely to be impaired.
An individual or a company in starting a manufacturing business would usually add to the capital they can
provide themselves, further sums borrowed in the form
of debentures secured on the business and yielding a
fixed rate of interest. The debenture interest being a
first charge, only such part of the value of the business
as corresponds to the profits of the proprietor or shareholders is available as the secondary security for temporary loans. But when the general level of prices is
falling, the value of the entire business will be falling
also, while the debenture and other liabilities, being
expressed in money, will remain unchanged. If the
business is earning £10,000 a year of which £7500 goes
in fixed charges, and if the general level of prices falls
5 per cent, the receipts will fall to £9500, but, the fixed
charges remaining the same, the profits accruing to the

proprietor or shareholders will drop from £2500 to
£2000, a fall of 20 per cent. Thus the amount of security
which can be offered from this source to safeguard
temporary loans is permanently diminished by 20 per
cent, while the amount of temporary loans needed is
diminished by only 5 per cent. But this is not the whole
story. For during the period of falling prices, the
expenses of production resist the downward tendency,
and the profits are temporarily diminished and may be
entirely obliterated or turned into an actual loss. A
weak business cannot bear this strain, and being unable to pay its debenture interest and having no further
assets on which to borrow, it will fail. If it is not re-
constructed but ceases operations altogether, that will
of course contribute to the general diminution of output. Its inability to meet its engagements will at the
same time inflict loss on the banks. But at present we
are considering credit, and credit depends on the
expectation of future solvency. A business which is
believed to be weak will have difficulty in borrowing,
because bankers fear that it may fail. At a time of
contracting trade the probability of any given business
failing will be increased. At the same time the probability of any particular venture for which it may
desire to borrow resulting in a loss instead of a profit
will likewise be increased. Consequently at such a
time credit will be impaired, but this will be the *consequence*, not the *cause* of the contracting trade.

There is nevertheless some tendency for this cause
also to exaggerate a contraction which has once begun.
For the mere reluctance of the banks to lend decreases
the quantity of credit money, independently of the
decrease occasioned by the rise in the rate of interest.

And it may be that when the banks have completed a sufficient contraction of credit money and lower the rate of interest to the level of the profit rate again, yet the amount of loans granted still continues to decrease.

At a time of expanding trade the fixed charges will become less and less burdensome on any business, and the margin available to pledge as security will increase. Bankers will be more confident of the solvency of would-be borrowers than before, and their confidence encourages them to lend more freely. Their willingness to lend increases the quantity of credit money, independently of the increase induced by the rate of interest being below the profit rate. Here, however, the tendency to lend will not last beyond the time when the banks have created as much credit money as they think reasonable. For whereas a bank will not lend to a trader whose solvency is doubtful, even if its existing liabilities are within the limit which it thinks prudent, yet it will be equally unwilling to lend to a trader of whose solvency it is satisfied if its liabilities are already up to that limit.

We may now proceed to consider the credit of the banker himself. We have already seen that the banker's estimate of the proper proportion of his reserve to his liabilities is almost entirely empirical, and that an arbitrary change in the proportion which he thinks fit to maintain between them will carry with it an increase or decrease, as the case may be, in the available amount of purchasing power in the community. If a banker really under-estimates the proper amount of reserve, and does not correct his estimate, he may find himself at a moment of strain with his reserve rapidly melting away and no prospect of the process coming to an end before

the reserve is exhausted. His natural remedy is to
borrow from other banks ; but this he can only do if
they believe his position to be sound. If they will not
lend, he must try to curtail his loans. But if he has
been lending imprudently, he will find that on his refusing to renew loans the borrowers will in some cases
become bankrupt and his money will be lost. It is
just when a banker has been lending imprudently that
his fellow-bankers will refuse to lend to him, and thus
the same mistake cuts him off simultaneously from the
two possible remedies. When a bank fails there is a
cancellation of the whole amount of purchasing power
represented by the loans outstanding at the moment of
failure. The people who have borrowed from the
defunct bank must either borrow from the surviving
banks to pay the loans back as they fall due, or they
must find the money by economising their expenditure.
The surviving banks cannot increase the aggregate of
their loans without any increase in their reserves, and
they must take steps to protect their reserves by raising
the rate of interest. Indeed, other banks which have
been sailing rather near the wind are likely to take
warning by the failure and to aim at a somewhat
higher standard in the matter of reserves. In short,
the aggregate of bankers' loans having been excessive
in comparison with the aggregate of legal tender currency, the former aggregate is diminished as soon as a
catastrophe gives practical demonstration of the necessity of such a step.

This preliminary investigation has shown at any rate
that changes in the aggregate of purchasing power, such
as may be the cause of fluctuations in trade, do actually
occur, and it thus affords *prima facie* proof of our theory.

But before passing on to deal with the complexities of
foreign trade, it will be convenient to touch upon the
kinds of disturbance which may arise in a self-contained
community from the conditions of production and consumption. We are only concerned with the effects of
such disturbances upon the state of trade as a whole,
not with the relative prosperity of the several branches
of trade.

If the demand for some commodity falls off, the
people engaged in the production of that commodity
will of course suffer. If a sum of £10,000,000 a year
is spent in hats, and if a craze suddenly develops for
going bareheaded, so that the sum so spent falls to
£8,000,000 a year, that means that the amount available to meet the profits, rents, interest, salaries, wages
of all the people directly or indirectly engaged in
supplying hats (so far as they derive their incomes from
that economic function), is reduced in the proportion
of £10,000,000 to £8,000,000. This reduction will make
itself felt first in the sale of hats by the retailers, and so
in the orders given by the retailers to the wholesale
dealers and manufacturers. The manufacturers must
either restrict their output or reduce their prices.
They can reduce their prices by sacrificing their profits,
but they cannot push the reduction appreciably further,
for that would require them to cut down wages. Wages
remain at their old level in all other branches of business.
Indeed, other branches of business gain what the hat
trade loses, for the £2,000,000 which would otherwise
have been spent on hats is spent on other things, either
on commodities for consumption or on the provision of
new capital. The bankers will see to it that the supply
of credit money is in due proportion to the supply of

cash, and that the diminished borrowings of the hat trade are made up by increased borrowings elsewhere. The effects, being widespread, will be relatively small, but such as they are they will take the form of an increase in the sales, and therefore in the prices of commodities other than hats, an increase in profits, an improvement in employment at the existing rates of wages, and a tendency for those rates to rise. Thus on the assumption that the supply of money remains unaffected, the depression of one trade, so far from tending to depress the others, tends rather to stimulate them. This will make it specially difficult for those engaged in the one trade affected to cut down wages, and therefore the principal effect of the depression will be a diminished output, throwing a portion of the employees out of work. These latter will be driven to look for other employment, usually either in unskilled trades, or in skilled trades more or less allied to their own, and of course it may be that some find themselves permanently incapable of earning a living. However, so long as the total stock of money remains unaltered the total of money incomes will be (practically) unaltered, and the industrial machine will continue to work steadily, even though there are thousands compulsorily idle and dependent upon charity or public assistance for their support. Those who, being in employment, are paying a portion of their earnings towards the maintenance of the unemployed are, of course, also suffering loss, but nevertheless the peculiar features of a general depression are not present.

In the contrary case of the growth of the demand for one commodity in comparison with the rest, there will of course be an increase of sales, an increase of output, an increase of prices, of profits, and of wages in the trade so stimulated. There will at the same time be a very slight depression in the other trades, and there will be a tendency for more capital and more labour than before to enter the trade in which profits and wages have risen. That is to say, the output in that trade will be gradually increased, and that of the other trades slightly diminished. But here again none of the characteristics of a change in the state of trade as a whole will be present.

In fact, it may be stated broadly that as long as the stock of money remains unchanged, a change in the demand[1] for some commodities as compared with the rest does not either stimulate or depress trade as a whole.

To pass next to changes in the conditions of supply, we will consider the effects of scarcity or abundance of food or raw material. The price of any commodity tends to rise or fall as the available supply falls or rises, and as the total amount of purchasing power available per unit of time to defray the cost of production of any kind of commodity is equal to the amount of the commodity purchased per unit of time multiplied by the price, the contrary movements of supply and price compensate one another's action. If the demand is elastic the price will rise or fall *less* than in proportion to the supply, if the demand is inelastic the price will rise or fall *more* than in proportion to the supply. An inelastic demand is usually characteristic of necessaries and an elastic demand of comforts or luxuries. For

---

[1] The "overproduction" of a commodity is the result of a miscalculated demand, and does not differ in principle from the case of a failing demand.

example, if the price of corn rises, people will hardly reduce their consumption of bread ; but if the price of umbrellas rises they will probably reduce their purchases of umbrellas very perceptibly.

The producers of a commodity for which the demand is elastic gain by an abundance and lose by a scarcity of the raw material. The producers of a commodity for which the demand is inelastic lose by an abundance and gain by a scarcity. The effect on the other trades of the community is in either case the contrary of the effect upon the trade under consideration, but, of course, except in the case of a very marked scarcity or abundance in a commodity of the first importance, this effect is likely to be inconsiderable. In the extreme case of a famine the total money expenditure on food will probably be much greater than usual, and as the aggregate money income of the community cannot increase so long as the money available to maintain the cash balances remains the same, the expenditure on all the other commodities will be diminished. This diminution of expenditure will of course involve a fall in prices and output, and there will result a loss of employment. But the enhanced receipts of those who are engaged in the supply of food will take the form of exceptional profits, and will not be accompanied by any increased demand on their part for labour. The farmers will perhaps continue to employ the same number of labourers as usual ; they certainly will not require more to deal with their diminished output, even though that diminished output represents a greater total money value than the full harvest of a normal year. The unemployed in other trades will therefore remain unemployed unless the rate of wages can be reduced. This represents a real trade depression, exhibiting all the features of a depression caused by a contraction in the supply of money, except that there is present a natural tendency to recover in the next year, or in the next year which produces a normal harvest, whether the various stages of adjustment are passed or not.

On the whole, the most remarkable feature of all these disturbances in demand or supply is that they have comparatively little effect on the state of trade. Except in the special instance of an actual famine, the fluctuations of demand or supply produce no fluctuations in trade as a whole, the depression or prosperity of one trade being compensated by the prosperity or depression of others.

VIII

A MONETARY DISTURBANCE IN AN INTERNATIONAL
SYSTEM WITH INDEPENDENT PAPER CURRENCIES

WE have now completed a sufficient survey of the nature
of fluctuations in a self-contained community, and it is
time to take the next step towards bringing the theory
into correspondence with the facts of the economic
world. This next step takes us into the midst of the
problems of international trade, and in order to deal
with the international aspects of fluctuations, it is
necessary to refer briefly to the underlying principles
of the foreign exchanges.

It will again be convenient, at the outset, to simplify
the problem by postulating an abstract world in which
some of the actual complexities are omitted, to be
introduced, one by one, at later stages. This abstract
world may be assumed to be a perfectly stable economic
system, composed of a number of independent countries,
each of which uses an inconvertible paper currency
which is not legal tender in any of the others. We will
also suppose that there are no protective tariffs.

In any country situated in this hypothetical world
there will presumably be a certain amount of foreign
trade. Now the transference of a cargo from one
country to another creates a debt due from some one
in the importing country to some one in the exporting
country. This debt cannot be discharged by the re-

mittance of money, because the two countries have been assumed not to use the same money. In fact, it cannot be paid at all unless there is some one in the exporting country who owes money to some one in the importing country. That the debt should remain outstanding or, in other words, that the total indebtedness of one country to the other should be permanently increased, is inconsistent with the preliminary assumption of perfect economic stability in all cases. So long as the condition of stability is maintained the indebtedness of the importing to the exporting country must be compensated by an indebtedness, accruing at an exactly equal rate, arising out of the transference of goods from the importing back to the exporting country. This statement requires qualification in two respects. First, the term " goods " must be regarded as including not only commodities, but also services. If a man in one country gives legal advice to a man in another, a debt is created exactly as if he had sent cheese instead of advice. Secondly, if one country is permanently indebted to another (a state not inconsistent with perfect stability) the borrowers will be permanently under the obligation of remitting the interest on the debts from time to time, as it falls due. In order that they may fulfil this obligation they must find in the creditor country people who need to pay money to the debtor country. Such people can only be found if there are exports from the debtor to the creditor country equal in value to the interest due, over and above any exports that are balanced by imports from the creditor to the debtor country.

We have, therefore, the principle that, so long as the condition of perfect stability is fulfilled, exports and

imports of goods and services pay for one another, and
that any excess of either over the other represents the
payment of a periodically accruing liability such as the
interest on borrowed money.

This principle requires us to equate together the
values of exports and imports reckoned in two independent currencies. It must be remembered that each
currency has been assumed to be inconvertible paper,
without intrinsic value, and owing its value in exchange
entirely to a domestic law which makes it legal tender
at home and has no validity abroad. The value of the
unit of either currency will depend merely upon the
amount which the Government has seen fit to issue in
comparison with the national needs for currency. How,
then, is the value of each unit in terms of the other
determined ?

The answer is to be found in the conditions under
which foreign trade is carried on. If goods are manufactured for export, the cost of production is measured
in the currency of the producing country, while the
producer can only draw upon the foreign dealer who
imports the goods in the currency of the dealer's own
country. In stable conditions the equivalent obtained
by the producer in the currency of his country for the
price received in the importing country must be equal
to the cost of production, which, in turn, is equal to the
price of similar goods in the producing country itself.
Moreover, wherever the supply of any goods is partly
domestic and partly foreign, the prices of the goods
derived from the two sources of supply must be identical. Also, no commodities can command a price in
either country greater than that of similar commodities
in the other by more than the cost of transporting them

unimpaired from the latter country to the former. These conditions all arise out of the existence of economic stability based on free competition. Between them they are sufficient to determine the relative values for the purposes of international payments of the respective units of currency of the two countries concerned.

The point of equilibrium in their trade will therefore be governed by the following principles. The cost of production of a commodity in either country, calculated in terms of labour and estimated on the assumption that the country supplies the whole of its own demand, would in general differ from that in the other. Any assumed rate of exchange between the two units of currency would afford a basis of comparison in terms of money between costs of production in the two countries, and the result would be to divide the products of each country into three classes: (1) commodities of which the money cost exceeds their money cost in the other country by more than the cost of transport, (2) commodities of which the money cost differs from their money cost in the other country by less than the cost of transport, and (3) commodities of which the money cost is less than the money cost in the other country by more than the cost of transport. Commodities of the intermediate class (2) would continue to be produced by each country for itself. But commodities of class (1) would be imported, and commodities of class (3) would be exported. If, in the case of any commodity of class (1), some of the producers are so favourably circumstanced that they can produce at a cost not greater than the cost of production abroad *plus* the cost of transport, then a part of the supply will continue to be provided at home by these producers.

Thus to any assumed rate of exchange there corresponds a determinate amount of exports and a determinate amount of imports, and, of all the possible rates of exchange, that alone will be consistent with economic stability which will lead to exact equality between exports and imports (or, if there is a net indebtedness of one country to the other, to such an excess of exports or imports as will just settle the accruing liabilities for interest). It is worthy of mention that the rate of exchange so arrived at, is entirely independent of any relation between the respective costs of production of any commodity in the two countries calculated in hours of labour and in the equivalent in hours of labour of the land, capital, and supervision employed. It may be that the industrial efficiency of one country is so far superior to that of the other that there is no single commodity produced by the second, but that the same commodity could be produced in the first and transported to the second at a less expenditure of labour and labour-equivalents. But if that is so, money wages in the more efficient country will be so much higher than the equivalent, at the prevailing rate of exchange, of money wages in the other as to preserve the equilibrium between exports and imports. For example, the superiority of Europe to India in industrial efficiency results not in a perpetual growth in the indebtedness of India to Europe, but in a great divergence between the money rates of wages. A European labourer can earn as many shillings in a day as an Indian can earn pence. Practically, it may be said that the rate of exchange equates the general level of prices of commodities in one country to that in the other. This is of course only approximately true, since the rate of exchange is affected only by those commodities which are or might be transported between the two countries. If one of the two countries is at a disadvantage in the production of commodities which cannot be imported, or indeed in those which can only be imported at a specially heavy cost, the general level of prices, calculated fairly over all commodities, will be higher in that country than in the other. But, subject to this important qualification, the rate of exchange under stable conditions does represent that ratio between the units of currency which makes the price-levels and therefore the purchasing powers of the two units equal.

Having indicated the conditions of a stable international economic system under the limitations assumed, we will now suppose the equilibrium to be disturbed. To begin with, it will be convenient, as in Chapter V, to assume that the countries concerned have no banking systems and no credit money. Let there be two such countries, A and B, and let a contraction of the currency occur in A. The immediate effects will be those which we have already traced in Chapter V. The cash balances of the community will be depleted, and there will be a curtailment of expenditure in order to restore them. The general restriction of expenditure involves a corresponding restriction in the sales of goods and services. The retailers find that they cannot get rid of their goods as quickly as usual, and they reduce their orders to the wholesale dealers and producers. The producers can only avoid restricting their output by lowering their prices; they accordingly lower their prices so far as the existing scale of their

expenses will permit. Their expenses depend mainly
on the rate of wages, and until the working population
will accept lower wages there must be some restriction
of output. This restriction of output represents the
adaptation of business to the contracted currency by a
reduction of volume instead of a reduction of money
values. In the remaining stage the pressure of distress
due to lack of employment drives the working class to
accept lower wages. As wages fall, prices fall, output
increases, and employment improves, until at last all
money values have completed a fall proportional to the
original diminution of the stock of money and equilibrium
is restored.

But the presence of another country, B, carrying on
commerce with A, necessitates a reconsideration of
this story. In the stable conditions preceding the contractions of the currency in A, there will have been an
exact balance of exports and imports. When the contraction occurs the exporters in B will find a diminution
in the orders for goods received from dealers in A, and
at the same time exporters in A will find a diminution
in the domestic demand for their products. In other
words, those classes of producers in either country who
are trading in both countries will find their business
in A diminished. They will no doubt reduce their
prices, both in A and B, in order as far as possible to
keep up their output, and the result will be that they
will sell more in B and less in A than before. Exports
from A to B will be increased, and imports from B to A
will be diminished. Imports will cease to pay for
exports, and a net indebtedness from B to A will be
created. How, then, is this indebtedness to be discharged ? It must be remembered that a creditor in

A cannot use the money of B, since both countries have been assumed to use independent inconvertible paper currencies. The actual practice of an exporter of goods to a foreign country is to draw a bill of exchange, which is documentary evidence that a sum of money is due to him in that country, and to sell this bill to a bill-broker in his own country, who will pay him for it the equivalent of the sum at the prevailing rate of exchange, less the necessary charges for discount, commission, etc. So long as exports and imports balance, the bill-brokers will find that the bills of either country on the other cancel out. But if the balance is disturbed this will no longer be so. If the exports from A increase and the imports decrease, the bill-brokers will find that in A they are paying out more money than they are receiving, while at the same time in B they will be receiving more money than they are paying out. Like other people engaged in business, bill-brokers must keep working balances of money, and the bill-brokers will find that their working balances in A are being depleted, and that their working balances in B are being inconveniently swollen. Steps must be taken to check these movements. Money cannot be sent from B to A ; it would be no use simply to increase the commission charged on every transaction, for though this would diminish the total volume of bill-discounting business the divergence between payments for exports and payments for imports would still exist. The only means of restoring the bill-brokers' balances is to alter the rate of exchange. The broker in A offers less of the currency of A for a given sum payable in B ; the broker in B offers more of the currency of B for a given sum payable in A. This makes the export trade from A to B less profitable, and the import trade from B to A more profitable, and a sufficient adjustment of the rate of exchange will make the two balance again.

To the question what precise adjustment will have this effect, there is no very simple answer. An alteration in exact proportion to the fall in the prices of commodities in A will not serve the purpose. Assume such an adjustment to be made. Then if the prices of commodities in B remained unaltered, the exporters of goods from A to B would get as much B-currency for them as before, but their receipts transformed into A currency will be reduced in proportion to the rate of exchange, i.e. in the same proportion as their receipts and the receipts of other producers from consumers in A. They will thus be able to maintain their export trade undiminished, and receive as much from goods exported as from goods sold at home.

On the other hand, exporters from B to A, though the reduced prices at which they sell their goods in A are equivalent to the same amount of B-currency as the old prices, will find that the quantity of goods exported is diminished, since the demand for commodities in A, even at the reduced prices, is lessened.

Thus the export trade of A will be maintained, while its import trade will be curtailed. No doubt the assumption made above that prices in B remain unaltered is not strictly correct. The exporters in A will suffer less from the slackening of demand than those producers whose entire market is confined to A, and they will therefore be inclined to make a less drastic reduction of prices, so that the prices of their goods in B-currency will tend actually to increase. The exporters in B, unlike other producers in B, will suffer some slackening of demand, and will presumably make some reduction of prices in B-currency in order to maintain output so far as they can. But both these tendencies only intensify the want of equilibrium between exports and imports, and it is clear that so long as the demand for commodities in A is below the normal the rate of exchange must be adjusted somewhat *more* than in proportion to the fall of prices in A. As the fall of prices continues, however, the demand for commodities in A grows, and the proportional discrepancy between the movement of prices and the movement of the rate of exchange will grow less, until at last, when the fall of prices is fully proportional to the initial diminution in the stock of money, the demand for commodities in A will have completely recovered, and the rate of exchange will again be in proportion to the purchasing powers of the two units of currency which it relates.

This theory of the adjustment of the rate of exchange is of course highly artificial and abstract. In order to bring it into relation with the facts it is necessary at once to proceed to deal with the operation of a banking system under the conditions assumed. Suppose, then, that both A and B possess banking systems, and suppose that a contraction in the amount of legal tender money occurs in A. The bankers in A will proceed to raise the rate of interest in A, in order to bring down the amount of credit money to a suitable proportion to the amount of legal tender money. There will of course be a slackening of demand, a curtailment of output, and a fall in the prices of commodities, with a tendency to produce all the consequences already described. But at the same time the increase of the rate of interest will have independent consequences equally important.

A man in B with money to spare for a temporary loan will be able to buy a bill of exchange on A, which will give him an equivalent sum in A. He can lend this sum at the high rate of interest there prevailing, and, when the loan matures, the money will be equivalent, owing to the change in the rate of exchange in the interval, to a *larger* sum in B-currency than before. The lender will thus make a profit on the exchange operations over and above the extra interest. If this opportunity is foreseen, people in B will hasten to take advantage of it ; there will be a demand for bills on A, and the rate of exchange will react to this demand ; the importation of goods from B to A will thus be stimulated, and A will become indebted to B. In fact, the future fall in the value of B-currency in terms of A-currency is anticipated, and the exporters of goods from B to A are enabled to undersell the producers in A, and thus to hasten that general fall of prices which is the necessary condition of equilibrium in A.

This process will continue until the requisite restriction of the volume of credit money has been accomplished. It should be remembered that the rate of interest only need be high relatively to the profit rate in A, which, under the influence of falling prices, will be less than the natural rate. As soon as the bankers are satisfied that their reserves and the amount of credit money are in due proportion, the rate of interest in A will revert to the profit rate, and the rate of exchange will then become subject to the laws which apply when there is no banking system.

During this final stage the profit rate in A will remain below the natural rate, and the market rate of interest will be equal to the profit rate. But a man in A with money to lend cannot take advantage of the higher rate of interest prevailing in B, where the profit rate is equal to the natural rate. For if he lends his money in B he will find when the loan becomes due that the rate of exchange will have changed to his disadvantage in the interval, and the net loss on exchange will eat up the extra interest. As a matter of fact this is only approximately true, for, as we have seen, the rate of exchange does not move exactly parallel with the prices of commodities in A. In the later stages of the disturbance the fall still to take place in the rate of exchange will be less than the fall still to take place in the general level of prices, and as it is on the latter that the depression of the profit rate depends, a lender in A will gain something by lending his money in B. But probably the inducement to do this will not be strong enough to be of much account.

From the above description, which is necessarily rather complicated, it will be seen that the mutual influence of two areas with independent currency systems is on the whole not very great. Indeed, the only important consequence to either of a contraction of currency in the other, is the tendency for the first to lend money to the second in order to get the benefit of the high rate of interest. This hastens the movement towards ultimate equilibrium in the area of stringency. At the same time it would raise the rate of interest slightly in the other country. But as this rise in the rate of interest is due to an enhanced *demand* for loans, it will not have the effect of diminishing the total stock of bankers' money.

It is hardly necessary to consider in the same detail the case of an inflation of the currency. The international effects (on the same assumptions as before)

correspond very closely with those which occur in the
case of a contraction. If the bankers find their reserves
to be above the necessary amount they relax the terms
for loans ; the aggregate of bankers' loans is increased ;
purchases are accelerated ; the producers increase their
output so far as possible, and prices rise. If the rate of
exchange remained the same as before, exports would
fall and imports would increase. The rate of exchange
must therefore be adjusted. If it were adjusted in strict
proportion to the rise of prices, imports would still be
increased in proportion to the general increase in consumption, while exports would be unchanged. Thus, so
far as the balance of exports and imports is concerned,
the adjustment of the rate of exchange must be a little
more than in proportion to the rise of prices. But
foreigners will be tempted by the low rate of interest
to borrow money, and the rate of exchange must be
further adjusted to check this tendency. It will thus be
pushed to a point at which there is an excess of exports
just equal to the amount of the loans being advanced
to foreign borrowers. When the low rate of interest
has done its work it will be raised again to the profit
rate (now above the natural rate owing to the rising
prices) ; the tendency to lend money abroad will cease ;
the rate of exchange will revert to the point determined
by the balance of exports and imports, that is, it will be
altered as compared with its original value a little more
than in proportion to the rise of prices which has occurred. From that point the gradual rise of wages will
begin to bring back the output in the area of inflation
to its normal level, and prices will rise a little further,
the rate of exchange being adjusted a little *less* than in
proportion to the rise of prices, until at last equilibrium

is restored, and all money values, as well as the rate of exchange, exhibit the same proportional change.

It is important to notice that as soon as the assumption of stable conditions is abandoned the rate of exchange ceases to represent the ratio of the purchasing powers of the two units of currency which it relates. A difference between the rates of interest in the two countries concerned displaces the rate of exchange from its normal position of equality with this ratio, in the same direction as if the purchasing power of the currency of the country with the higher rate of interest had been increased. Such a divergence between the rates of interest would only occur in case of some financial disturbance, and though such disturbances, great or small, are bound to be frequent, the ratio of purchasing powers may still be taken (subject to the qualification previously explained) to be the normal significance of the rate of exchange.

IX

A MONETARY DISTURBANCE IN AN INTERNATIONAL SYSTEM WITH A COMMON METALLIC MEDIUM OF EXCHANGE

THE foregoing exposition relates of course to a hypothetical world. But it is best to approach the problems of international trade at first by making the assumptions therein adopted, for inconvertible paper currencies, having no real " par " of exchange, exhibit the true character of the rate of exchange much better than metallic currencies. We have shown that the rate of exchange tends to represent simply the ratio of the purchasing power of the two units of currency, and that when this ratio is disturbed, the rate of exchange, subject to certain fluctuations, follows it.

But having elucidated this point we can now pass to the much more important case of the international effects of a fluctuation experienced in a country using a metal currency common to itself and its neighbours. Practically all the great commercial nations of the world have now adopted gold as their standard of legal tender, and this completely alters the problem.

This establishment of gold as the monetary standard means not merely the use of gold coins, but the free coinage of gold. The Government undertakes to turn into coin any quantity of gold which may be brought for the purpose, and either charges nothing or charges the bare cost of the process.

Where these conditions exist, gold bullion which can be turned into coin at any time is practically as good as gold coin. The coin in virtue of its quality of being legal tender will often command a slight premium, but this premium will not be greater than the cost of coining *plus* interest for the period occupied by the process. These arrangements amount practically to the use of the same standard of value by all the gold-using countries, just as if they had an international unit.

As it is still the effects, not the causes, of a contraction or inflation of the currency which we are investigating, we will again assume some arbitrary change in the circulation. Suppose, for instance, that in one country some step is suddenly taken which has the effect of completely withdrawing a large quantity of gold from circulation.[1]

The first effect will of course be a depletion of the bankers' reserves, and the bankers will promptly respond by raising the rate of interest. The result of raising the rate of interest is, as we have seen, to attract loans from abroad, and the borrowers by drawing bills on the lenders and getting them discounted will diminish the bill-brokers' balances in the area of stringency. The bill-brokers will defend themselves by altering the rate of exchange, but here arises the fundamental difference from the case of independent inconvertible paper currencies. For it is possible for a lender to put his gold in a box and consign it direct to the borrower without resorting to the use of bills at all, and if the rate of exchange passes a certain point it will become more

[1] It does not matter precisely what the step is. If the reader desires a concrete illustration he may suppose that the gold is melted down and made into a calf for the people to worship.

profitable to do this than for the borrower to draw a bill on the lender. The point at which the consignment of metal becomes profitable is called the " specie point." It is reached when the quantity of gold which can be obtained by discounting a bill of exchange is less than the quantity equivalent to the sum expressed on the face of the bill not only by the interest up to the date of the bill's maturity, but in addition by the whole of the charges for freight, etc., payable on the carriage of the metal.

For instance, if these charges for the remittance of gold from London to Paris, or from Paris to London, amount to ½ per cent of the sum remitted, and if the gold in £1 is equal to the gold in 25·22 francs, then when the exchange for cheques (for which there is no discount) is at about 25·09 a man in Paris can have £10,000 in gold sent to him from London, equivalent to 252,200 francs, and pay 1261 francs for freight, etc., leaving 250,939 francs in his hands, whereas if he had drawn a bill on his debtor in London he would have got 250,900 francs only. There are two specie points in the exchange between any two places. When it is profitable to send gold from London to Paris, the London exchange on Paris is said to have reached the " export specie point," and the Paris exchange on London to have reached the " import specie point." When it is profitable to send gold from Paris to London the situation is exactly reversed. On the assumption made above as to the cost of remittance the specie points would be approximately 25·09 and 25·35.

In the case, then, when a high rate of interest is attracting loans from abroad to any considerable extent the bill-brokers will quickly put down the exchange to import specie point, and gold will flow in from abroad. This will begin at the same time to fill up the bankers' reserves at home and to deplete those abroad. The foreign bankers must in turn protect their reserves by putting up the rate of interest in their respective countries. Thus the contraction of the currency at once tends to spread itself over the whole of the gold-using world. The consequent depression is by this means alleviated in the area of stringency, but only at the cost of being extended in some degree to all the other countries.

The foreign bankers will not raise their respective rates of interest immediately, or will not raise them so high as absolutely to prevent gold being withdrawn. If they did they would soon find their outstanding loans diminished and their reserves unnecessarily enlarged. They are prepared to let some gold be withdrawn, but must so far raise the rate of interest as to ensure a simultaneous reduction in loans.

The reduction in loans will be gradual, and their proper course is to adjust the rate of interest in such a way that the reduction of loans and the withdrawals of gold shall just about keep pace. As the foreign lenders have to meet the cost of sending their gold before they can get the benefit of the high rate of interest the foreign rates of interest will be a little lower than the rate in the area of stringency, and the difference will be the greater the more distant the foreign country. We might trace each great trade route or line of communication and find the prevailing interest lower and lower, as the distance and the cost of carriage of gold grow greater and greater. If the contraction was slight and the consequent rise in the domestic rate of interest correspondingly small, it might be that the exchange with the more distant foreign countries would never touch the specie point at all.

Consider, then, the case of any selected foreign country. If it is so distant and the disturbance so slight that no gold is imported from it the conditions approximate to those already examined, where independent inconvertible paper currencies are employed. The extent and anticipated duration of the rise in the rate of interest in the area of stringency are not sufficient to meet the cost of actually remitting gold. The tendency in the selected foreign country to take advantage of the rise by lending money can be confined within limits by an adjustment of the rate of exchange short of the specie point. This adjustment will induce a balance of imports from the foreign country, and the equilibrium position must be such that loans equal to the value of this balance of imports will also be made. In other words, the exchange not having reached the specie point, any sum borrowed passes in the form of goods.

If, on the other hand, the selected foreign country is near enough and the monetary disturbance great enough to cause an actual movement of gold, the rate of exchange must be forced up to the specie point. This adjustment of the rate of exchange will of itself, as in the previous instance, induce a balance of imports from the foreign country to the area of stringency, and a portion of the foreign loans will thus come in the form of goods. But over and above this balance of imported goods a greater or less amount of gold will be sent. There will be a rise in the rate of interest in the foreign country, but not so great as the rise in the rate of interest in the area of stringency. In either case the rise in the rate of interest will have its normal effects of discouraging loans, diminishing the aggregate of purchasing power, curtailing purchases, retarding output, and reducing prices. But, other things being equal, these effects will be less marked in the foreign country since the rise in the rate of interest is there less. There will be a tendency therefore for imports into the area of stringency to be checked by the falling demand and the drop in prices, while the same causes will stimulate exports from that area to the foreign country. If independent currencies were used, this tendency would result merely in an adjustment of the rate of exchange. But as gold is used in both countries and the exchange is already at the specie point, the excess of exports from the area of stringency cannot be checked by this means and must be met by a further transfer of gold. That is to say, the effect of the discrepancy in prices in the two countries is to cause a greater portion of the foreign loans to come into the area of stringency in the form of gold instead of in the form of goods. Indeed, if the discrepancy of prices were very pronounced and the transport of gold cheap, the imports of gold might actually be greater than the total of the foreign loans.

When the bankers' reserves in the area of stringency are restored the rate of interest reverts to the profit rate. The bankers' loans in the foreign country may be supposed to have been gradually diminished in proportion to the stock of gold, the rate of interest having been adjusted to make them keep pace. There is no longer any tendency for money to be lent from the foreign country to the area of stringency, but the discrepancy of prices still exists and will cause a continuance of the flow of gold into the area of stringency to pay for the excess of exports therefrom. In order to produce a continuance of the corresponding reduction in the bankers' loans in the foreign country the rate of interest there must continue to be something above the profit rate. On the other hand, in the area of stringency loans can be actually increased in proportion to the new gold imported, and the rate of interest there could even be reduced below the profit rate. An intelligent anticipation of this situation would lead the bankers to reduce the rate of interest to the profit rate before the restoration of their reserves is completed, and to trust to the continued influx of gold to place them finally in a sound position during this later stage. So long as the flow of gold continues the total purchasing power in the foreign country will be diminishing, and the total of purchasing power in the area of stringency will be increasing. The tendency towards an excess of exports from the latter to the former will thus be steadily losing force, until at last the difference in the prices of commodities in the two areas is so far reduced that the excess of exports is checked altogether by the rate of exchange being fixed just at the specie point. When this stage is reached the flow of gold will cease, but the rate of exchange will not react appreciably from the specie point. Equilibrium will be reached with a lower level of prices in the area of stringency than in the foreign country ; just so much lower as to maintain the rate of exchange up to the specie point, but not past it.

It must be borne in mind that the rate of exchange, so long as it is *within* the specie points, represents practically the ratio between the average levels of gold prices in the two countries which it relates, just as the rate of exchange between independent inconvertible paper currencies practically represents this ratio between the average levels of paper prices. If the exchange between London and Paris is at par (which we will take to be 25·22 francs to £1), and if the quantity of gold in France is increased by ¼ per cent, then, after affairs have been adjusted, the exchange will have risen to 25·283. Prices in France will on an average be simply ¼ per cent higher than before, but the English prices of French goods will be unaltered, and the French prices of English goods will have risen in the same proportion as French incomes and the French prices of French goods. It is only when the divergence of prices is so great that the corresponding adjustment of the rate of exchange would push it beyond the specie point that any gold passes. Thus, as soon as the flow of gold has depressed the prices of commodities in the selected foreign country so far that the percentage by which they exceed the prices of commodities in the area of stringency is not greater than the percentage representing the charges for the transport of a given sum of gold, the flow of gold will stop.

The principles governing the rate of exchange may be illustrated by the following mechanical example. Represent two countries by two cisterns, and their stock of legal tender money by water, so that the depth of the water in either cistern may be taken to be the general level of prices in the corresponding country. If water cannot pass from either cistern to the other any divergence of depth may be produced at will by adjusting the respective quantities of water in them. This corresponds to the case of countries with independent currencies. If, however, the water can flow through a pipe leading from the base of one cistern to the base of the other, the depths in the two cisterns will always be identical. This does not correspond strictly to the case of gold-using countries, because gold does not flow quite freely from one to the other, and a difference of depth corresponding to the specie points must be possible. This can be represented if the pipe be supposed to contain a valve which will prevent the flow of water unless it is subject to a certain pressure, but which under that pressure from *either* side will open. When a difference of level exists great enough to cause this pressure upon the valve, water will pass through the pipe until the difference of level has been reduced to a point at which the pressure is no longer sufficient to keep the valve open. The rate of interest must be represented by some mechanical means of adjusting the pressure in either cistern, a rise in the rate being equivalent to a diminution of pressure which would tend to suck in water from the other cistern.

This mechanical example may be extended to represent any number of countries by an equal number of cisterns each of which must communicate through valves with all the others. It may be supposed that water is being poured from an external source into some of these cisterns, which will represent the gold-producing countries, and from which it will be distributed through the valves to the others. Every cistern must also be assumed subject to artificial means of altering the pressures of the water in it, representing not only adjustments of the rate of interest, but also all other changes in economic conditions which may affect the need for currency.

To return, however, to the consideration of the effects

of a contraction of the currency in a country forming
part of an international gold-using system. It will be
observed that, in the course of the process described
above, the area of stringency becomes indebted to the
selected foreign country, the new indebtedness representing the loans attracted from it during the period
of high interest. These loans would be for short periods,
and we cannot assume that equilibrium has been
restored until we have considered what will happen
when they fall due. First of all, it is at any rate clear
that the loans will not be repaid in gold. The exchange
is at the import specie point, and no one will go to the
expense of paying the freight and insurance on a consignment of gold to a foreign country when by the purchase
of a bill he can get a greater quantity of gold placed to
his credit there without any such expense. The foreign
creditor may receive his money from a bill-broker, who
will be entitled to receive the equivalent at the prevailing rate of exchange from the debtor in the debtor's
own country. The bill-broker will find his cash balance
in the creditor's country diminished and his cash
balance in the debtor's country increased. He could,
no doubt, correct the tendency by adjusting the rate
of exchange and offering less money in the creditor's
country as the equivalent of a given sum in the debtor's
country. This adjustment of the rate of exchange
would discourage the export of goods from the creditor's
country to the debtor's country, and encourage the
export of goods from the debtor's country to the
creditor's country. But the presumption is that this
course will not be taken. The money placed in the hands
of the creditor is ready for investment. The debtor has
probably found it necessary to borrow elsewhere the

whole, or the greater part, of the money which he paid
to the bill-broker. The ordinary process of the renewal
and replacement of capital in both countries will have
been resumed when the price-movement was completed,
and, apart from the creditor's action in calling in his
loan, would progress at the same rate as before the
disturbance in both, and in both would yield interest
at the old natural rate. It follows that, as a consequence
of the calling in of the loan, there is rather more money
seeking investment in the creditor's country and
rather less in the debtor's country than there was before
the disturbance. This situation will be reflected in the
relative prices of similar securities in the two countries,
and the bill-broker will find it profitable to take advantage of this and to apply the money which he received
from the debtor to investments made on the spot.
The result will be that the renewal and replacement of
capital in the two countries will keep pace, but that the
foreign indebtedness of the country in which the
monetary stringency originated will have been permanently increased. In other words, the calling in of
the loan has no effect on the relative indebtedness of
the two countries at all. Indeed, it should be pointed
out that the process of renewal and replacement of
capital is retarded during a depression and there will
probably be some shortage of capital in the area of
stringency, as compared with foreign countries, when
the depression is over. If this is so the openings for
investment there will be slightly more profitable than
usual, and there will actually be some further growth in
its foreign indebtedness.

The effects of a contraction of the currency of a gold-
using country in a gold-using international system may

be summarised as follows : Gold flows from foreign countries to the area of stringency in response to the high rate of interest, more quickly from the nearer and more slowly from the more distant countries. While this process is at work the rates of interest in foreign countries are raised, more in the nearer and less in the more distant countries. As soon as the bankers' loans have been brought into the proper proportion to the stock of gold, the rate of interest reverts to the profit rate in the area of stringency, but the influx of gold continues from each foreign country until the average level of prices there has so far fallen that its divergence from the average level of prices in the area of stringency is no longer great enough to cover the cost of sending the gold.

So long as any country is actually exporting gold the rate of interest will there be maintained somewhat above the profit rate, so as to diminish the total amount of bankers' loans *pari passu* with the stock of gold.

At the time when the export of gold ceases from any foreign country the rate of exchange in that country on the area of stringency is at the export specie point ; and the exchange will remain at this point indefinitely unless some new influence arises to disturb the equilibrium. In fact, the whole economic system will, in the absence of such influence, revert to the stable conditions from which it started.

These may be taken to be, broadly, the stages of the process by which a contraction of the currency in one country reacts on the others. There are still some details, however, which require to be filled in.

During the first stage, when high interest prevails in the area of stringency, and the rate of interest is raised, though to a less extent, in the neighbouring countries, every country will experience some fall in prices, and there will be a tendency on the whole for the greatest fall to be recorded in those which are nearest and in which for that reason the rise of the rate of interest is greatest.

But though we can say that in given conditions the greater the rise in the rate of interest above the profit rate the more pronounced will be the fall in prices, yet in the various foreign countries the conditions cannot be assumed to be uniform. In some of them wages and prices will be more sensitive to changes in the total of purchasing power than in others. Suppose, then, that in one country a given rate of withdrawal of gold depresses wages and prices more quickly than in the others. Initially the rate of interest must be raised to the point which maintains the due proportion between the bankers' reserves and their outstanding loans, and a determinate rate of outflow of gold will ensue. But we have seen that in addition to the outflow of gold on account of loans, there is a further outflow towards the area of stringency due to the fact that the more rapid fall of prices in that area increases its exports and decreases imports. If prices fall more quickly than is normal in the selected foreign country, this latter outflow of gold will be checked, or even possibly reversed, and by this cause the divergence of the fall of prices from the normal rate will be diminished.

Thus, in general, those countries in which wages and prices are more sensitive to a diminution of purchasing power will tend to lose less gold, and those in which wages and prices resist a reduction will tend to lose more gold than would otherwise be the case. At the end of the first phase, when the bankers' reserves are restored to equilibrium in the area of stringency and the rate of interest reverts to the profit rate, the fall of prices will still continue. But those countries which have experienced a less proportional loss of gold will reach equilibrium at an earlier period and at a higher scale of prices than those which have experienced a greater proportional loss. This equilibrium cannot persist, for the balance of exports and imports between the two classes of countries will be upset, and gold must pass to settle the difference.

In fact, in the earlier stages gold is drawn more especially from those countries where wages and prices resist change, and in the later stages their extra loss of gold is recouped from those countries in which wages and prices have responded more readily. The fluctuation is therefore sudden and violent in the former, and gradual and mild in the latter.

This completes our examination of the effects of an isolated and abrupt contraction of the currency in one among several gold-using countries. It is unnecessary to describe in detail the effects of an isolated and abrupt inflation occurring under the same conditions. It is enough to say that the superfluous gold will flow from the area of inflation to the surrounding countries, that all the effects of an inflation as already described will be present in an intenser degree in the area of inflation and in a milder degree in the other countries in proportion to their distance therefrom.

In the foregoing investigation we have ruled out the complications which may arise from protective tariffs. The effects of the imposition of a new tariff or of the repeal or alteration of an existing tariff will be examined at a later stage when we come to consider the possible causes of fluctuations in an international system. At present we are only concerned with the influence exerted upon a given fluctuation by protective tariffs which are assumed to remain unchanged throughout its progress.

We will now revert to the simple case of two countries with independent inconvertible paper currencies, and we will suppose one of them to have a protective tariff. Before dealing with a fluctuation in such a case we must be prepared to revise in some respects the theory previously enunciated of the rate of exchange.

In that theory the rate of exchange afforded a basis for comparing the costs of production, expressed in money, of commodities in the two countries. With that basis of comparison the products of each country fall into three classes : (1) those of which the money cost exceeds their money cost in the other country by more than the cost of transport, (2) those of which the money cost differs from the money cost in the other country by less than the cost of transport, and (3) those of which the money cost is less than their money cost in the other country by more than the cost of transport. The rate of exchange between the respective units of currency was then seen to be such that the value of the goods of class (1) imported must just balance the value of goods of class (3) exported, subject to the necessary correction for other liabilities, such as interest on borrowed capital.

If, however, one of the two countries levies duties on imported goods, then for that country the goods of class (1), which are of course for the other country the goods of class (3), must be confined to those of which the cost of production exceeds their cost of production in the other country by at least the cost of freight *plus* duty. This will of course diminish the amount of goods in class (1) and increase those in class (2), leaving class (3) unchanged. Therefore the rate of exchange which would produce equilibrium under free trade conditions will not do. The unit of currency in the protected country must be equivalent to rather more units of the currency of the free trade country. This will increase the money cost of production of all commodities in the protected country expressed in the currency of the free trade country. Some goods which could at the free trade rate of exchange have been profitably exported will fall back into class (2), while some which, under the protective tariff and with the free trade rate of exchange, would have passed from class (1) to class (2), will with the adjusted rate of exchange be retained in class (1) and be profitably imported. The most conspicuous effect is to diminish the total volume of international trade, the exports from the protected country being in the end affected in the same degree as the imports into it.

The rate of exchange between the two countries no longer expresses the relative purchasing powers of their respective units of currency. Even under free trade conditions this is only approximately true, for the prices of the same commodity in the two countries may differ by any amount not exceeding the cost of transporting it from either to the other. Any commodity will be cheaper in the exporting than in the importing country, and in the case of some commodities the cost of transport forms a very large proportion of the cost of production ; but, as exports and imports balance, the rate of exchange will very nearly express the ratio of purchasing power.

Where, however, there is a protective tariff, imported goods will command prices representing the equivalent of their cost of production *plus* the cost of transport *plus* the customs duty. And in some trades, though the effect of the tariff will be to prevent any goods being imported, prices will yet exceed (though by less than the duty) the equivalent of the cost of production abroad *plus* the cost of transport.

If of two countries one has no tariff and the other has a tariff of 20 per cent on imported goods, then the goods exported from the former to the latter will be 20 per cent dearer (apart from freight) in the protected country than in the free trade country, while the goods exported from the protected country to the free trade country will (apart from freight) be at the same price in both. Other goods may be dearer in the protected country by any amount not exceeding 20 per cent (together with freight). Probably, therefore, the ratio of purchasing power will differ by something comparable to 10 per cent from the rate of exchange.

In the case of gold-using countries it is still true that the rate of exchange cannot pass the specie point. Therefore, in order to maintain the higher level of prices there must be in a protected country a proportionately greater supply of gold.

Subject to these observations very little alteration requires to be made on account of the existence of protective tariffs in the description already given of the effects of a depression in an international system. If from any cause the stock of purchasing power in one country is diminished, the other countries will tend to export gold to make up the deficiency. This tendency only ceases when the other countries have suffered such a diminution of purchasing power, and the area of stringency has made such a corresponding gain of purchasing power, that their prices for foreign trade purposes no longer differ so much as to keep the exchange beyond the specie point. The prices of goods for foreign trade purposes will therefore have fallen in approximately the same proportion everywhere, subject to the margin allowed by the cost of remitting gold. For example, if the prices at the area of stringency have fallen 5 per cent, then in a country from which the cost of remitting a sum in gold is $\frac{1}{2}$ per cent they will have fallen $4\frac{1}{2}$ per cent, or in a country from which the cost of remitting is 1 per cent they will have fallen 4 per cent. But in a country with a protective tariff equivalent on an average to 50 per cent of the value of the imported goods, and involving a difference of, say, 25 per cent in the average level of internal prices, the effect on internal prices may be different from the effect on prices for the purpose of foreign trade. If the tariff is composed of *ad valorem* duties, then, as the prices of imports fall, the duties will fall, and the proportional fall of prices will be exactly the same as under free trade. But if the tariff is composed of specific duties, i.e. of duties assessed at so much per unit of quantity of each kind of goods taxed, then the fall of internal prices will be less than in proportion to the fall of foreign trade prices. For instance, if prices in the area of stringency have fallen 5 per cent, and if the cost of remitting gold is 1 per cent, the prices of the exports and imports between the protected country and that area will be diminished by 4 per cent. But the duties still remain equal to 50 per cent of the old level of prices of imported goods. The foreign trade prices have dropped from 100 to 96, but the prices of imported goods have only fallen from 150 to 146, and the general level of internal prices from 125 to 121, or 3·2 per cent. The reason of this is that the old duties are made slightly more protective by the enhanced value of the gold in which they are paid.

It is also necessary to notice that a greater quantity of gold is required to produce a given proportional change in the level of prices in a protected than in a free country. Fluctuations arising out of the banking system will therefore have greater international consequences, if they occur in a protected than in a free trade country.

X

SOCIAL AND ECONOMIC CHANGES

WE started to consider the problem of fluctuations in an abstract community, without banks, and without neighbours. We have now removed these limitations and so proceeded from the abstract towards the concrete. One other limitation remains. We have assumed that apart from a single isolated cause of disturbance the economic conditions have been and would continue to be perfectly stable.

To bring our theory into touch with the actual conditions of the world we must remove this last limitation. This means that we must take into consideration all those economic changes, whether progressive or transitory, which arise from social and industrial causes. We find an increasing population, with an increasing output and an increasing accumulated store of material wealth. We also find habits and tastes and productive methods changing.

The growing population, in spreading over the earth's surface, is guided by its own convenience. For the due organisation of human endeavour, men must be near one another. Therefore new communities are founded preferably in those places from which there is readiest communication with the centres of civilisation already in existence. A new community requires from its very beginning to be furnished with a certain minimum of accumulated wealth or capital. Its members must have houses, furniture, clothes, and a preliminary stock of food and perishable necessaries. The area occupied must be opened up with harbours, roads, and railways and other lines of communication, and a supply of ships, vehicles, rolling stock, etc., must be provided. And for whatever industry is to be carried on, whether agriculture, mining, or manufactures, the necessary plant, including buildings and machinery, must be set up.

The new communities grow out of the old as branches from a tree. It is only by intercourse with the old communities that the new can provide themselves with the necessary stock of capital. And, like a tree, a human colony takes root. Once the preliminary stock of fixed capital has been created it can only be deserted at a heavy sacrifice. The population of the world are always committed to using the fixed capital and inhabiting the dwellings which already exist. The amount of labour involved in the building of new towns and the making of new lines of communication is so great that no very extensive change can be made except gradually and over a long period of time.

Every year, however, the population of the world increases by several millions, for whom as they grow up new fixed capital has to be provided. The places where this new fixed capital is set up are chosen for many reasons. On the one hand, the needs of social, political, and economic organisation prompt the new generation to settle as near as they can to the centres of population from which they have sprung. On the other hand, the growing population requires an ever-increasing supply of natural products, organic and inorganic. Under the

influence of the former cause each year's accretion of
adult population tends to build itself streets, shops, and
houses in the most accessible places in the immediate
neighbourhood of an existing town or village.   Under
the influence of the latter they tend to migrate to places
of which the natural resources are still undeveloped.
By the one tendency they are concentrated, by the
other scattered.

Nevertheless, the scattering tendency is always
governed by the necessity for communication.   New
areas are first brought under cultivation to supply the
needs of the communities already in existence ; they
must be able to import from those communities the
wealth necessary to capitalise their undertakings, and
they must be able to export their own products in repayment.   Therefore at any moment only those areas
which are within reasonable reach of existing lines of
communication are being developed.   Moreover lines of
communication, whether roads and railways or harbours
and ships, are not indefinitely and capriciously extended.   They represent a vast amount of concentrated
labour, which the world can only afford to expend when
some substantial economic gain (as measured against
the gain which might be derived from an alternative
application of the labour) will be realised.

When colonists penetrate into a new area to develop
its natural resources, they quickly reproduce the social
conditions to which they have been accustomed.   They
find it necessary to create markets at the points at
which it is convenient to collect their produce for
export ; and these points, chosen for convenience of
communication with the interior of the colony and with
the outside world, are for the same reasons the most

convenient headquarters for political, economic, and
social organisation. The result is that even in the
process of scattering over the undeveloped area they
create new points of concentration.

There still remains, however, a marked difference
between a "new" country and an "old" country.
The new country is less thickly populated in proportion
to its natural resources. From that it follows that the
new country can supply itself with food and raw
materials at a less cost of labour than the old. Each new
line of communication is a conduit through which the
resources of the area into which it penetrates flow out
into the world. Thus the new countries, on the whole,
export food and raw materials to the old. The old
countries must export manufactures in return.

As we have seen, the development of a new country
is limited by the rate at which capital can be provided.
If the new country were isolated and self-contained,
only a limited portion of its productive power could be
applied to capital expenditure. To maintain the in-
habitants in health and reasonable comfort a certain
portion of the annual output must take the form of
commodities ready for consumption, and only the surplus of productive power, remaining available after
these commodities have been provided for, can be
applied to capital extensions. The fact that a great
part of the commodities required for consumption can
be imported sets free a corresponding part of the
country's productive power for capital extensions, and
the capital extensions can be still further accelerated
by the importation of machinery and other commodities for use in production.

In order to obtain this supply of capital the new

country must be prepared to compete with the capital requirements of the old. In the old country there are openings for investment in providing for the needs of that part of the increment of population which remains at home, as well as in improving and extending existing economic enterprises. But all these exist in the new country in due proportion to the amount of population and industrial enterprise already to be found there; and in addition there are the openings offered by projects of new lines of communication with an undeveloped interior, or of the further development of the country to which existing lines of communication have only recently penetrated.

Thus the old and more populous country is usually in the position of exporting capital to the new and less populous country. It should be remarked, however, that the development of the new country presupposes a certain continuance of immigration. It is no use putting fixed capital into the new country unless labour is forthcoming to man the fixed capital when it is completed. The first colonists will man the initial supply of fixed capital, but thereafter the development of the country will need both further supplies of colonists and further supplies of capital.

Besides these phenomena of the steady growth of wealth and population, there are innumerable other sources of economic change. Some work in the same direction over long periods of time, such as the growth of technical knowledge and the consequent improvement in productive processes. Others are only temporary, such as changes of habits and tastes. For the most part these need not be considered in detail. But before facing our main problem of how fluctuations are brought about by the circumstances of the actual world, it will be useful to examine for a moment the practical conditions under which the supply of currency is carried on.

Hitherto we have assumed an arbitrary change in the available stock of currency as the starting-point of our investigations, and we must satisfy ourselves whether such changes may play an important part in practice as well as in theory. The great commercial nations of the world, as we have seen, employ a gold standard. Most other nations either employ a gold standard or use paper or overvalued silver of which the gold value is kept as steady as possible by a careful regulation of issues and withdrawals. A few states of slight economic importance use inconvertible paper of no fixed metal value. China almost alone adheres to a silver standard. Thus the world's supply of currency practically means the world's supply of gold.

If other commercial, industrial, and banking conditions are to remain substantially unchanged, it is evident that the annual supply of gold must keep pace with the growth of population in the gold-using countries. If that population increased by 1 per cent per annum and there were no fresh supply of gold, then prices would fall by 1 per cent per annum, and the rate of interest for any loan for a period over which these conditions were expected to continue would be 1 per cent below the natural rate. To maintain the average level of prices and incomes unaltered the stock of gold in the world must increase at the same rate as the population. Gold is practically indestructible, and the annual amount withdrawn by loss or wear from the total stock is small. The annual production of gold in the world, though it may vary, is always more than sufficient to cover the decrease due to these causes.

Materials do not exist for making any very trustworthy estimate of the stock of gold in the world and the proportion thereto of the annual production. The stock of gold in use as coin, or as bullion practically taking the place of coin, is probably from £1,250,000,000 to £1,500,000,000. I know of no estimate of the amount in use as plate, jewellery, and for other such purposes. About twenty years ago the annual production had fallen off, and reached a minimum of below £20,000,000. With the development of the South African and other mines, and improvements in the processes of gold mining, the production has risen steadily and now exceeds £90,000,000 a year. These statistics go far to explain the low rate of interest which prevailed in the 'eighties (when in this country the debt was successfully converted) and in the 'nineties (when Consols rose to 113⅞) as compared with the high rate which has prevailed in recent years when all gilt-edged securities have been falling continuously. Such vagaries in the annual gold supply are very important. But the changes usually occur over such long periods that trade accommodates itself to them almost insensibly, and they do not of themselves cause alternations of " good " and " bad " trade. We shall find it necessary to return to this subject in a subsequent chapter.

A country which produces gold will export the gold to that place at which it will command the highest price. The price received for the gold will take the form of a payment for a bill at the prevailing rate of exchange on the place to which the gold is sent. The place selected as the destination of the gold will be that on which the rate of exchange is at the highest premium. A gold-producing country is of course saturated with gold, and exchange on any foreign country is likely to be at a premium. As the rate of exchange represents approximately the relative purchasing power of gold in the two areas between which it obtains, this premium will be highest in the case of exchange on that country in which the purchasing power of gold is for the time being greatest. In other words, gold flows from the gold-producing country to those places at which for the time being there is the greatest scarcity of gold. This scarcity may occur in a new country the immigrant population of which requires to be supplied with currency as with all other forms of material wealth ; a part of the new gold must also be distributed among the old countries, where the population may be assumed to be growing, though no doubt less rapidly than in the new. But though in the long run it will be used to meet the needs of the additional population, the immediate movements of the gold will be determined by the state of the exchanges for the time being, and it may wander through several countries lying under the shadow of temporary depressions before it finds its ultimate destination.

This process is noteworthy in that the flow of gold from the mines to the places where there is a scarcity of purchasing power tends to relieve the stringency at those places without draining the existing stock of gold away from the neighbouring areas. But though the movements of new gold influence trade fluctuations in this and other ways, only exceptional and sudden changes in the gold supply, such as the discovery of rich new mines, would actually *cause* fluctuations. And even when such changes occur their consequences must be worked out in conjunction with those of the many other causes which are likely to be operating in the same or the contrary direction.

XI

FLUCTUATIONS OF SUPPLY AND DEMAND

In Chapter VII we have already seen the manner in which a trade fluctuation may arise in an isolated community through an imperfect adjustment in the banking system, and we there considered the effects in the same direction of various changes in the conditions of production and consumption. The upshot was that, whereas the influences arising out of the banking system are very important, those which arise from the conditions of production and consumption have but little bearing (except perhaps in the case of actual famine) upon the state of trade as a whole. In reopening in the wider field of an international system the question of how fluctuations are caused, we must review the conclusions reached in that chapter.

It will be convenient to deal with the conditions of production first. In Chapter VII we traced the consequences of changes first in the demand and then in the supply of a single commodity. To extend the argument from the isolated community to the international system we must now consider the effect on one country of changes in the demand for its products in another. To begin with, we will again simplify the problem by assuming that there is no international metallic medium of exchange, but that each country has its own inconvertible paper currency. Suppose, then, that there is a diminution in the world's demand for some specified commodity, for instance, hats. If every country supplied its own demand for hats and no more, the effects of this diminution would be practically the same as in a self-contained community. The case now to be examined is that in which there is some foreign trade in hats. Given that a country has an export trade in hats, what will be the effect upon it and its neighbours if the demand for hats is diminished ?

The falling demand will first make itself felt in a slackening of the retailers' business. This will be spread uniformly over all countries. The retailers will then give smaller orders to the wholesale dealers and manufacturers, and the manufacturers will reduce their prices in order so far as possible to maintain their output and keep their plant and labour employed. As other trades are *ex hypothesi* enjoying the same demand as before, the general level of wages will be maintained, and it will be more difficult than in a time of general depression to reduce wages in the hat trade. But whatever the exact process of adjustment may be, the net result will of course be that the gross receipts of the hat business will be less than before, and there will ensue the following consequences :—

(1) The balance of international trade will be disturbed, the exports of the hat-producing country having been diminished.

(2) The hat manufacturers' business will be carried on on a smaller scale. They will need smaller balances with their bankers to pay (*a*) for less raw material, etc., (*b*) a smaller wages bill, (*c*) smaller profits and dividends.

(3) The hat manufacturers will need at any time a smaller volume of outstanding loans to finance their restricted business.

(4) The workmen in the hat trade will be fewer and will probably receive somewhat lower wages, and will therefore hold a smaller aggregate amount of cash in their pockets and their money-boxes.

The three last-named processes may be all summed up under the single heading of a diminished share of the hat trade in the resources of the money market, and it remains to follow out still further the adjustments consequential on this and on the disturbance of the balance of international trade.

Exports from the country we are considering cease to be sufficient to pay for imports. Money which under the preceding conditions the bill-brokers would have been using to discount the hat manufacturers' bills begins to accumulate in their hands. This tendency they counter by altering the rate of exchange, so as to give more money at home in exchange for a given sum abroad. The effect is to encourage exports (relieving somewhat, but of course not entirely, the depression of the hat trade) and to discourage imports. The bill-brokers' balances then no longer accumulate, and the accumulations (representing the hat manufacturers' loss in respect of the gross receipts of their foreign trade) are dissipated among the rest of the community. In fact, the increase in the prices of imported goods (reckoned in the domestic currency) necessarily involves increased prices and an increased output of the domestic goods with which they compete.

The increased financial needs of trades other than the hat trade will therefore absorb the money and credit set free by the diminished demand for hats. While this process is at work the profits of these trades will be enhanced by rising prices, and the manufacturers and others engaged in them will be in a position to offer a correspondingly high rate of interest for loans. The hat manufacturers, meanwhile, will be making very low profits or will be working at a loss, until the restriction of output has reached the point at which the retail prices of hats are sufficient to pay all expenses of production including the maintenance of such portion of the existing plant as remains in use. A position of temporary equilibrium will be reached, in which the money value of commodities other than hats, and money wages in trades other than the hat trade, have been increased, but the labour displaced from the hat trade is still unemployed, and the superfluous capital embarked in the hat trade is idle. If the hat trade never recovers, the superfluous capital is permanently wasted, and represents a dead loss to the community. The superfluous labour will no doubt to a great extent be gradually absorbed. But the special skill of the workmen displaced will be wasted. The absorption of the superfluous labour will be accompanied by a corresponding increase in the output of commodities and a corresponding fall in money prices and money wages. When the process is completed money wages and money prices will have been put back to the level at which they stood before the depression in the hat trade, but

(1) The accumulation of capital will have been retarded.

(2) The productive resources of the country will (presumably) be less profitably applied than before.

(3) The foreign trade of the country will (probably) be permanently diminished in volume, and the rate of exchange permanently displaced.

There is no reason to suppose that any serious banking disturbance would necessarily or even probably be occasioned at any stage. The collapse of an important industry may no doubt cause a shock to general credit. If the collapse is attended with the bankruptcy of individual firms, it may be that banks which have specialised in financing the industry are involved in their fall, and that the credit of firms mainly engaged in other business, but still substantially interested in it, is so shaken that they are for the moment unable to borrow. A curtailment of credit money might ensue, which would bring with it all the phenomena of depression and perhaps even of crisis.

It is frequently argued that the depression of one trade in a country tends to cause depression in the others, inasmuch as the purchasing power of the people engaged in the trade immediately affected is diminished and they are therefore not in a position to buy so much as before of the goods produced by their neighbours. It should be noted that in the circumstances assumed this argument is not valid. The quantity of money in the country is *ex hypothesi* undiminished and the structure of incomes built upon this money as a foundation is, or at any rate may be presumed to be, unaltered. The change that has taken place is this, that the incomes are in slightly fewer hands than before, the workmen who have lost employment having lost along with it their right to share in the national resources. When a small portion of the working classes become destitute, and the part of the national money income which they have been receiving is distributed partly among the remainder of the working classes and partly among the owners of property, there may be some slight changes in the relative demand for different commodities. But the aggregate demand for commodities remains unaltered and if the demand for some falls off the demand for the remainder is correspondingly stimulated.

But this applies only to the case where there is no international currency. It still remains to examine the case of a system of gold-using countries.

Assume again the same example as before, a hat-exporting country exposed to the effects of a fall in the demand for hats, but suppose that it and its neighbours use a gold currency. The slackening demand will of course make itself felt, as in the previous case, through two tendencies :—

(1) An adjustment of the exchange " against " the hat-exporting country.
(2) A diminution in the money (cash and credit) in the hands of the hat business.

But if the disturbance is appreciable the rate of exchange may go up to the specie point, and there will then be a tendency to export gold to pay for the excess of imports arising from the diminished export of hats. Now the bankers cannot submit to an export of gold without taking steps to bring down their loans to a proper proportion to the supply of gold which will be

left in the country. They will raise the rate of interest
with the following consequences :—

(1) There will be a tendency on the part of foreign
countries to lend, i.e. the liability arising from
the excess of imports will be left for the moment
in whole or in part outstanding.

(2) Borrowers will be discouraged and the aggregate
of bankers' loans will be diminished.

(3) The bankers' gold reserves will begin to increase.
The bankers will therefore soon have gold to
spare, and will reduce the rate of interest again
so far as to permit some gold to be exported.

How far will this export of gold go ? Suppose that
the manufacture of hats represents $\frac{1}{2}$ per cent of the
world's production of commodities, services, etc., but
that it represents 10 per cent of the production of the
hat-exporting country. Suppose, further, that the
demand for hats is diminished by $\frac{1}{5}$, i.e. that the amount
spent by the world on hats is $\frac{4}{5}$ of what it was. The
diminished production of hats represents $\frac{2}{5}$ per cent
instead of $\frac{1}{2}$ per cent of the world's production, and
8 per cent (approximately) instead of 10 per cent of the
production of the hat-exporting country. Taking the
gold-using world as a whole, if the total value of the
gold used as currency and bank reserves is £1,500,000,000,
$\frac{1}{2}$ per cent of that sum or £7,500,000 may be earmarked
as the gold needed to finance the hat trade before the
depression began, this sum including of course not only
the reserves held by the banks against the accounts
of the hat-making firms, but the gold in the pockets
of all the people whose incomes are derived from

making hats or dealing in hats. If the demand for hats falls by $\frac{1}{5}$, then, after the necessary adjustments, the sum needed to finance the hat trade will have fallen to £6,000,000 and the gold available for all other business will have risen from £1,492,500,000 to £1,494,000,000, or about $\frac{1}{10}$ per cent. If the hat-exporting country has £25,000,000 of gold currency, then £2,500,000 of this will be needed to finance the hat trade before the depression and £2,000,000 afterwards. If there were no export of gold, the gold available for other industries would rise from £22,500,000 to £23,000,000, or rather over 2 per cent, and prices in those industries would rise approximately in the same ratio. This would only be possible if the rate of exchange (which apart from special causes of disturbance represents practically the relative purchasing power of gold in the two regions it relates) could rise by 2 per cent. Assume that the cost of exporting gold to the nearest foreign country would be $\frac{1}{2}$ per cent. Then the exchange cannot rise by more than $\frac{1}{2}$ per cent. Of the £500,000 of gold surrendered by the hat trade only so much can be retained in the country as will raise the £22,500,000 employed in financing other businesses by $\frac{1}{2}$ per cent, i.e. £112,500. The remaining £387,500 must be exported (*except* for a trifling proportion which can be retained because there is an increase of about $\frac{1}{10}$ per cent in the world's supply of currency for businesses other than the hat trade).

But even so equilibrium is not yet reached. For the export of hats has been diminished by 20 per cent, and if the prices ruling in other industries are the same, relatively to those ruling abroad, as before, the imports of those commodities will be unchanged. There must therefore be a further export of gold to lower the general level of prices and so to encourage exports and discourage imports.

Thus the loss of gold is traceable to two distinct causes. First of all there is the loss proportional to the definite diminution in production, and therefore in the national income, through a portion of the capital and labour in the hat-making industry being left idle. *Secondly,* there is a further loss corresponding to the further diminution in the national wealth consequent upon the trade affected being an export trade and therefore one for which the exporting country was specially suited. In order to restore the balance of trade, commodities which it is less specially suited to produce must be exported, and this is made possible by the further depletion of the stock of gold and by the corresponding reduction of money values and of money cost of production.

There follows the final stage in which the displaced labour is gradually absorbed into other industries. As this process goes on, the gold sent away will be steadily attracted back, thus avoiding the element of falling prices and consequent depression which would mark the corresponding stage under a local inconvertible currency.

It might at first sight be supposed that under the conditions here postulated it is broadly true to say that the depression of one industry is communicated to the others. It is the case that the export of gold prevents these other industries being actually stimulated. But nevertheless, it is not true that they share the depression. For the curtailment of exports leads to a corresponding curtailment of imports. The diminution of the purchasing power of the persons engaged in the industry affected is measured by that very curtailment of exports, and is just compensated by the increased domestic demand for commodities arising from the curtailment of imports.

We thus arrive at the conclusion that a diminution of demand in one industry, though it may cause heavy losses and great distress, will not in general affect other industries adversely and will not, in fact, produce a *general* trade depression.

After considering in detail the effects of a curtailment of demand for any commodity in an international system it is hardly necessary to deal at length with the effects of an expansion of demand, since the latter phenomenon differs little from a mere reversal of the former. It will therefore be more profitable to proceed at once to consider the effects in an international system of influences bearing upon the *production* of a commodity.

The causes affecting production may be either local or general. Climatic irregularities, political disturbances, labour troubles, discoveries of new sources of supply, are usually local. But some of these may be world-wide in their operation ; and some causes are usually of universal operation, such as the invention of improved processes. It will be simplest to begin with a universal influence, and proceed afterwards to the consideration of a local influence. We assume the influence to be universal in the sense that it affects equally all sources of production. Those sources of production must be supposed to be unequally distributed among the different communities which constitute the international system ; otherwise the problem would not differ appreciably from that of the self-contained or isolated community. But the local distribution of the processes of production has nowadays become highly complex. There are many stages in the production of a single finished article ; the different stages may take place in widely distant places ; the same raw material may enter into the production of many different commodities. A cause affecting production may act upon the supply of the raw material, or on any of the subsequent processes. For the sake of simplicity we will start by assuming that the commodity concerned is brought up to a certain definite stage of manufacture at its place of origin and that the remaining stages are invariably completed in the country in which it is to be consumed, so that the goods in transit are always at the same uniform stage of manufacture. We shall thus be concerned only with the local distribution of the producers in the producing countries, and of the consumers (with their attendant producers) throughout the international system, and there will be no intermediate manufacturers with a different local distribution to complicate the problem.

Now let some influence operate to diminish the output of the commodity to be obtained from the given economic agencies, in the form of labour, capital, and land, devoted to its production. We saw in Chapter VII that the effect of this on the market must depend on whether the demand for the commodity is " elastic " or " inelastic." In the former case when the cost of production and therefore the price rises the aggregate sum spent by the consumers upon the commodity *diminishes*, in the latter case the aggregate sum so spent *increases*.

The first effects of the diminution of output will be

that at existing prices the receipts from sales will no longer be sufficient to pay the expenses of production, while at the same time the manufacturers can no longer keep pace with the orders of the wholesale dealers. There must, therefore, at once be an increase of price, and the character of the demand will determine how far the increase of price can go. If the demand is elastic the increase will stop before the aggregate receipts from sales have reverted to the previous figure ; if the demand is inelastic the increase will be sufficient to carry the aggregate receipts beyond the previous figure. In either case the subsequent phenomena are very similar to those which occur when it is the demand for a commodity which is directly affected, the former case corresponding to a flagging demand, the latter to an expanding demand. It is therefore unnecessary to trace in detail the various developments ; the decrease (or increase) of the financial requirements of the industry affected ; the passage of gold to (or from) that industry from (or to) other industries ; the consequent export (or import) of gold from (or into) the producing countries ; or the incidental effects on the balance of trade and the rate of exchange. The only important difference is that the diminution of the quantity of the commodity obtained by a given expenditure of economic effort must be written off as a clear loss before the effects of the change in demand are taken into account at all. In just the same way the effects of increased production will correspond, according as the demand is elastic or inelastic, with those of increased or decreased demand. And of all these occurrences it is uniformly true that outside the particular business directly affected there is no trade fluctuation properly so called, or at any rate none of material importance. An exception is to be found in the case of actual famine, where (as in the case of a self-contained community) the reaction upon other industries becomes considerable. But the production of the necessaries of life is so widely distributed over the world that a world-wide famine is very unlikely to occur. The effects of a scarcity of raw material on the manufacturing communities, as distinguished from the producing communities, are of course excluded by our hypothesis.

This hypothesis can now be removed, and intermediate processes of manufacture having a local distribution different both from that of the production of the raw material and from that of the consumption of the finished product may be admitted to consideration. How, then, will a locality, which imports the raw or incomplete article and exports it after applying to it one of these intermediate processes, be affected by an increase or decrease in the supply of the raw material? Consider first a decrease. A continuance of work at the existing rate will begin to deplete the stocks of raw material. Those stocks cannot be replenished as quickly as before, and consequently the manufacturers will curtail the orders which they will accept from the wholesale dealers. This restriction in supply will elicit from the consumer a higher retail price, and the wholesale dealers will thus be enabled to offer a higher price to the manufacturers, who in turn can offer a higher price for the raw materials and so get an increased supply (though not, of course, equal to the old supply, otherwise the higher retail price could not be maintained). Under conditions of free competition, the manufacturers would find their plant and their hands underemployed, and would be willing to accept a price just sufficient to cover the cost of raw material *plus* working expenses. This would still be so, even if the demand were inelastic, so that the aggregate receipts from sales of the finished product were actually greater than before the scarcity. The whole advantage of these increased receipts would be passed on to the producers of the raw material. In fact, whether the demand is elastic or inelastic there will always be a diminution of output, and the manufacturing communities will suffer both by having less work and by earning less for the work they have. In other words, they experience precisely the results which would follow a contraction of demand.

All the foregoing examples of causes affecting production have been confined to cases where the operation of the cause is uniform in its effects over the entire production of the commodity concerned. A further complication arises where the disturbance is local. For example, how will a country be affected by an exceptionally good or exceptionally bad harvest ? It is a commonplace of the money market that a country which has a good harvest in any year will need money and, if a gold-using country, will need gold. The distinguishing feature of a local variation in production is that it does not have the same effect on prices as a world-wide variation affecting the entire production of one commodity. Thus a good harvest in one country has usually relatively little influence in diminishing world prices. The elasticity or inelasticity of demand becomes a matter of minor importance and the money value of the harvest in the world's markets is more or less proportional to its volume.

When the harvest is reaped and comes into the market there will be a greater surplus for export (or a smaller deficiency to be made up by imports) than in a normal year, and there will thus arise a balance of indebtedness from foreign countries. The farmers may invest part of their exceptional profits abroad, but part, at any rate, they will either spend or invest at home, and as the money comes to be remitted to them for that purpose the bill-brokers will find their balances diminishing and will adjust the rate of exchange towards and probably up to the import specie point. Sufficient gold will then be imported to raise prices and stimulate imports up to the point at which they pay for the exceptional exports, or at any rate for such portion of those exports as cannot be set off against exceptional investments abroad. This importation of gold may begin before the harvest is actually reaped. For as soon as the exceptional yield is foreseen the farmers will want to borrow more money than usual to pay for the cost of reaping, carrying, etc., and the bankers will be ready to lend more than usual in anticipation of the farmers' swollen profits. But the bankers must have larger supplies of gold to support the increased loans ; they will raise the rate of interest and will so attract gold from abroad. When the whole harvest has been disposed of and sufficient imports have been obtained in exchange, the surplus gold will be sent abroad again.

It should be observed that the gold is not imported from abroad to discharge the balance of indebtedness *directly*. Indeed, as it is not ultimately retained it does not affect the balance of indebtedness in the long run at all. The balance of indebtedness is discharged by the increased importation of goods, and only so much gold need be imported as will stimulate imports in the required degree.

Incidentally the importation of gold also stimulates domestic trade, so that the good harvest reacts favourably for the time being on the general state of trade in the country. But the contrary effect is experienced when the gold is sent abroad again later on and prices return to their old level.

Just as an exceptionally good harvest necessitates the import of gold, so will an exceptionally poor harvest lead to the export of gold. And, of course, if production is checked or stimulated in any other way the effect is the same. For example, a prolonged labour dispute will diminish the financial needs of the industry affected. The industry will not be in a position to undertake new orders (which would involve new borrowings), and though loans already obtained for existing orders will in many cases have to be in part renewed, the employers will not be paying their usual weekly wages bills; they will, on the whole, be able to diminish materially their outstanding indebtedness, and will draw much less cash than usual against their current accounts. At the same time the workmen will be subsisting on strike pay, savings, and credit, and their weekly budgets will be less than when they are receiving their full earnings. The average amount of cash in their pockets will be correspondingly less. Taking the personnel of the industry as a whole, therefore, they will in the course of the dispute part with a great portion of the cash and credit money which is ordinarily in their hands. The cash set free will tend to stimulate other industries, to push up the rate of exchange, and, if the dispute is important and prolonged, to find its way abroad. When work is resumed, of course, the employers will want to borrow again the sums necessary to finance the orders, the execution of which has been interrupted, and the cash exported will be rapidly attracted back.

Here, then, as in other cases, it seems that disturbances arising from the conditions of supply and demand, as distinguished from financial disturbances, always tend to have a strictly limited effect. It is only rarely that they influence to any serious extent industries outside those directly touched.

Even with so widespread a disturbance as the recent coal strike, although a considerable section of the industry of the country was almost completely paralysed, yet outside the business directly dependent on the supply of coal the effect was unexpectedly slight, and the recovery of trade when it was over was remarkable.

XII

PREVALENT FORMS OF CREDIT MONEY

On the whole the results of the last chapter may be regarded as negative. The economic disturbances therein
examined all have a relatively slight and transient effect
on the state of trade. The effective causes of trade
fluctuations must be looked for in the sensitive and
omnipresent machinery of money and credit. Here
we have already found such causes in considering the
case of an isolated community in Chapter VII, and
we have now to extend the reasoning which formed the
subject of the first portion of that chapter to the more
complex case of an international system.

It then appeared that the most important cause
of fluctuations was to be found in the failure of the
bankers to keep proper control over the creation of
credit money. Firstly, when money is lent to a trader
an interval elapses before the corresponding demand for
cash matures, and before, therefore, the full effect of
an increase of loans in depleting the bankers' cash
reserves is felt ; and *per contra* when the bankers curtail their loans an interval will elapse before a proportional amount of cash is attracted back. Secondly,
it was shown that a banker's failure to adjust his lending
operations correctly to the needs of the market tends
to produce a cumulative effect which will be steadily
accelerated unless timely steps are taken to reverse it ;

a mere increase in the amount of bankers' loans of itself leads to an increase in the demand for loans on the existing terms.

Thirdly, bankers may be tempted to lend imprudently, and when their rashness finds them out, whether they pay the penalty in bankruptcy, or whether they manage to restore their business to a sound footing, in either case a quantity of credit money will have to be annihilated.

Up to this point we have dealt with banks in a highly abstract and generalised form. We have assumed that the banker has made himself liable to pay money on demand, and that the right to obtain money on demand is given in such a form as to be a convenient substitute for cash to the possessor of the right. This is the essence of the process of creating banker's money or " credit money." But in considering how the system works in practice there is much more to be taken into account, and in the present chapter we shall examine in a little more detail the prevalent types of banking law and practice.

If credit money is to be a convenient substitute for cash, any one who has obtained a supply of credit money from a bank must be in a position to pay it away to other people. This may be effected in one of two ways, either by bank-note or by cheque.

A bank-note is a transferable document issued by the banker entitling the holder to obtain on demand a sum specified on its face. The problem of effecting payments in credit money is solved by the simple process of handing on the document itself.

Under the cheque system the banker places to his customer's credit a certain sum, but gives him no transferable documentary evidence of the existence of this sum. But the customer can at any time direct the banker to pay any portion of the money to any third person. The direction is given in writing, and the handing over of the written document or cheque to this third person is, for practical purposes, the equivalent of a payment.

It is not necessary to enlarge on the differences between the two systems. The acceptability of the bank-note depends on confidence in the genuineness of the document and in the solvency of the issuing bank. The acceptability of the cheque depends mainly on confidence in the honesty of the man who writes it. The bank-note may circulate many times from hand to hand : the cheque is usually (though not necessarily) employed for one transaction only. The bank-note may be for any sum, large or small, but is not divisible ; the cheque may be made out for the precise sum required for any transaction.

But for all these differences, there remains the fundamental identity of the right to draw any sum by cheque with the possession of bank-notes representing in aggregate value the same sum. Either is simply the possession of so much credit money, and from the point of view of the banker means the liability to pay that sum on demand. All that has been said in the preceding chapters on the subject of credit money applies impartially to both systems.

But it does not follow that there are not important practical differences between the two kinds of credit money, even from the point of view from which we are now interested in the subject of banking. The most important of all arise from the fact that notes have a closer resemblance than cheques to cash. Indeed, there is really no hard-and-fast line between cash and notes at all—only a continuous gradation from bullion at one end, through legal tender full-valued coin, legal tender overvalued coin, legal tender inconvertible notes, legal tender convertible notes, finally to convertible notes that are not legal tender. Bullion derives its value solely from its own nature; full-valued coin adds to its intrinsic value the advantage of express legal recognition; overvalued coin has little, and inconvertible notes have nothing, to boast of but their legal standing; legal tender convertible notes have a legal standing so long only as they represent faithfully something other than themselves; and convertible notes that are not legal tender have no virtue in themselves at all, but are merely documentary evidence of some assets elsewhere.

Moreover, the quality of being legal tender is itself variable. A bank-note may be legal tender for all purposes or only for certain specified transactions, e.g. it may be legal tender for the payment of taxes, but not for any other transactions, or it may be legal tender so long only as the issuing bank complies with certain conditions. Again, convertible notes may be ordinary credit money secured by such cash and other assets as the banker thinks it prudent to hold against them, or they may be subject to various statutory or other restrictions, prescribing the proportion of cash that must be held or the character of the other assets, or limiting the total amount of the notes that may be issued. The most completely circumscribed form of paper money is what may be called the " gold certificate," where the entire note-issue is secured by a reserve of cash equal to its face value. In such a case there is no profit on the issue, and a banker will not therefore undertake it as part of his business. Gold certificates can in practice only be issued either by Governments or by banks which are willing to issue them in exchange for some special privilege, and which are practically the agents of the Government for the purpose. An issue of this kind serves the purpose of providing a more portable form of currency for large transactions, and of saving the gold deposited from the attrition which would result from use. Neither this nor any other form of note-issue has the advantage of a current account operated on by cheque in dispensing the holder from any precautions against loss or theft. It is true that notes are usually made identifiable by means of serial numbers, and are therefore easier to trace than coins ; but, on the other hand, they are destructible. On the whole, therefore, the gold certificate has very little advantage over coin beyond its portability.

A gold certificate is not credit money at all. There are some forms of note-issue, however, which in practice hardly differ from gold certificates, but which yet are in a sense credit money. An example is to be found in the Bank of England note. The Bank has the right to issue a certain fixed amount of notes (at present £18,450,000) against securities, but can only issue notes in excess of that amount in exchange for cash or gold bullion, which when received must be held in reserve, and cannot be drawn upon for any other purpose than cashing notes. Consequently, for the purpose of any increase or decrease in the note-issue, the Bank of England notes are practically mere gold certificates ;

they would only assume the characteristics of credit money, in being expansible or contractible independently of the supply of gold, if the amount of the issue fell to a point near £18,450,000.

In the case of gold certificates, the convertibility of which is absolutely secured, the question of the legal-tender privilege is of little importance. As they are issued by the Government or under Government auspices, they are naturally in practice made legal tender, but so long as the entire issue is known to be secured by cash they will in any case be freely accepted.

In the case of an ordinary bank-note, however, the legal-tender privilege is a matter of considerable importance. The convertibility of the note depends upon the prudence and honesty of the issuing bank, and if it is not legal tender it is valueless apart from its convertibility. In a community where the banks have an unrestricted power of note-issue, no one will accept a note unless he is satisfied that the issuing bank is solvent, or at any rate no one will accept a note if he has any reason to doubt the solvency of the issuing bank.

The writer of a cheque has personal knowledge of the bank on which it is drawn ; the recipient of the cheque pays it into his own banking account, and it is presented at once by his bank for payment through the clearing-house. The interval between the writing and the realisation of the cheque is so short that the chance of the bank becoming insolvent is infinitesimal, and even if the bank did fail to meet the cheque the drawer would remain liable for the money. This is a very important difference between the bank-note system and the cheque system. In the former case the individual holder possesses credit money in the form of bank-notes giving him the right to receive money on demand, it may be, from a number of different banks, of the solvency of which he, and the people to whom he wishes to make payments, may have very slender information. In the latter case he has the right to receive money on demand from one selected bank which he knows and to which he is known, and that right cannot be exercised except by his personal intervention in the form of a written authority. The relation of bank to note-holder is an impersonal one ; the relation of bank to depositor is a personal one.

The note-holder regards his notes as simply money, and if in doubt of the solvency of any of the issuing banks, is perfectly ready, at very little sacrifice of convenience, to use actual money instead. The depositor values his relation with his banker ; if he happens to have an unnecessarily large balance he knows that it is not entirely wasted, for he is thereby acquiring merit in his banker's eyes ; he will not lightly draw out his balance, even as a precaution when doubt is thrown on the banker's solvency ; nor will he lightly transfer his account to another banker who is not acquainted with his affairs. Thus the personal relation of banker and depositor is a great safeguard against the embarrassing demands which may be made upon a bank in consequence of distrust. This safeguard is largely absent in the case of the note-holder, to whom the bank-note is a mere convenience like a gold certificate. The result is that while the demands of depositors are regulated by the real needs of business, the demands of note-holders are subject to capricious fluctuations which may arise at any time from a loss of confidence in the issuing banks.

Again, a banking account is, on the whole, the privilege of the man of substance. A bank-note for a small sum will get into the hands of people of small means. The inconvenience of withdrawing a large balance in cash is serious ; but there is no such inconvenience to deter the small note-holder from demanding cash at any time.

All these differences may be summed up in the single statement that bank-notes have much more of the character of cash than a balance at a bank operated on by cheque.

In the history of banking the bank-note for a long time held a much more important place than the cheque system. So long as the bank-note was the prevailing form of credit money, one of the most important problems which vexed the minds of bankers was the maintenance of confidence. There could be no profit on a note-issue unless the cash in reserve were less than the amount of the issue. Yet in that case it was indisputable that if the note-holders all chose to present the notes for payment at the same time the bank would fail to cash all. And if the note-holders were aware of this how could they feel enough confidence to abstain from doing that very thing ?

As a matter of fact the portability of notes was a sufficient inducement to the public to use them, and so long as every one was confident that the general use of notes would continue, there was no reason for any individual to fear a universal run on banks of issue. But nevertheless experience did show that the bank-note was an unstable form of credit money, and that a slight loss of credit by an individual bank might lead to its complete collapse. The result has been a continuous growth of Government control of banks of issue. In some cases the note-issue has been made a statutory monopoly of a single bank, which is practically a Government Department. In some, again, stringent conditions as to the proportion of the cash reserves to the notes in circulation have been laid down, amounting in the case of the Bank of England, for instance, almost to the conversion of the note into a gold certificate. In many cases the nature of the securities to be held against the portion of the issue not covered by cash has been prescribed, for example, in the United States, where the National Banks are allowed only to issue notes covered by United States Government Bonds, and their issues are limited, therefore, by the amount of Government debt outstanding. In most cases the bank-notes which are allowed to circulate have been made legal tender for some or all purposes.

Nearly everywhere the proportion of cash reserve to note-issue is required to be very much higher than would be thought reasonable for the cash reserve held against deposits. The result is that the bank-note has come to take second place as a basis for the creation of credit money. The amount of credit money which can be created by this means from a given quantity of gold is relatively small. And so great are the precautions taken to safeguard modern issues, that the notes are practically regarded as cash, and themselves form the foundation on which a far larger superstructure of credit money is set up in the form of deposits.

One result of the development of the cheque system is that the demands on a bank for cash are much less affected than formerly by the state of its credit. Depositors draw out cash not because they are afraid the bank is going to collapse, but because they want cash for some purpose, such as the payment of wages, for which cheques would not be suitable. Their needs for cash follow fairly well-defined laws, and bankers endeavour to foresee the operation of those laws and to provide cash accordingly. There is some tendency still to attribute too much importance in the theory of finance and banking to the state of credit. For example, it happens, when bankers have been creating credit money too freely, that their cash reserves begin to fall away, and the rate of interest has to be promptly raised. It is sometimes assumed that the demand for cash and the high rate of interest are both signs of loss of confidence. To the reader who has followed the preceding chapters it is hardly necessary to point out that the bankers raise the rate of interest, not because they distrust the borrowers, but because they are afraid that if the manufacture of credit money continues unabated the corresponding demand for cash, which is bound to follow, will exhaust their reserves. This may happen even though there is never any breath of suspicion against the soundness of any bank or business firm.

It is hardly too much to say that the normal working of the machinery of the money market cannot be understood until the relatively subordinate part played by the impairment of credit, that is to say, by the expectation that banks or other businesses will fail to meet their engagements, is fully realised. A contraction or depression of trade is ordinarily accompanied by a number of failures, especially if it be started by a commercial crisis. But even a crisis cannot be fully explained by a general loss of confidence. A crisis only differs in degree from an ordinary contraction of trade. The manufacture of credit money has so far outstripped the due proportion to the supply of cash that recovery is only possible by means of immediate and drastic steps. The loss of confidence may be very widespread, but it is still only a symptom and not a cause of the collapse.

XIII

After the survey in the preceding chapter of the different kinds of credit money in use, we are now in a position to consider some of the leading principles of national banking organisation so far as they bear on our subject. To these principles we adverted very briefly in Chapter III, but any examination of them in detail was postponed, and in the intervening chapters we have always assumed the banks to respond as a whole to the various influences of the money market. In Chapter III it was mentioned that most of the great commercial nations have adopted the system of a central bank, more or less intimately associated with the Government, with full responsibility for the national gold reserve. To this rule there is one very important exception, the United States, but it will be convenient to deal first with the central bank system as giving most clearly the essentials of banking organisation.

The great central banks of the European nations usually combine with their responsibility for the national gold reserve either a monopoly of note-issue or at any rate a predominant position as banks of issue. This dual function introduces complexity into the subject, and it will therefore be best to begin with the English system, where the note-issue is of subordinate importance. The English system of note-issue differs from that of most other countries in two respects. First, there are no notes of a value below £5, while silver is not legal tender for payments above £2 ; consequently, gold coins cannot be completely replaced by notes for the payments for which cheques will not serve and a large quantity of gold is necessarily in circulation outside the banks. Secondly, as we have already seen, the Bank of England note is very little more than a gold certificate, inasmuch as no additional notes above a fixed amount can be issued unless an equal amount of gold is added to the reserve of the issue department, which is kept for the sole purpose of cashing notes. Under the English system, therefore, the bank-note is not a means of creating *additional* credit money at all, but exists merely to avoid the inconvenience of handling large sums in gold.

The Bank of England thus exemplifies the central bank system practically free from the complications arising from the manufacture of credit money by note-issue. The essence of the system is that all banks other than the central bank confine their holdings of legal tender money to the sums required as working balances for their ordinary daily needs. They rely on obtaining further supplies from the central bank whenever there is a danger of their running short, and when their holdings of legal tender money grow larger than they think necessary they deposit the superfluous balance in the central bank. In fact, these banks do not maintain a " reserve " at all, in the sense of a large sum in gold set apart for emergencies, and remaining untouched throughout long periods of normal business conditions. They keep sufficient " till money " to enable them to supply the regular needs of their customers, and they have their own balances on current account or on deposit at the central bank. These balances, which are necessary to enable them to draw on the central bank when occasion arises, they regard as " reserves " ; but from the point of view of the central bank these balances are deposits like those of any other customer, only a proportion of which need be covered by actual legal tender money.

Perhaps in an ideal system the central bank would confine itself strictly to its business as the bankers' bank, and would not accept deposits from private individuals at all. In actual systems this is not so. The Bank of England receives deposits from persons and businesses other than banks, and in particular from the Government. The position of the Government in England and elsewhere as a large depositor in the central bank raises important questions to which we will return later. But for all that the essential function of the Bank of England is to be the bank with which all banks bank.

In our previous discussions of the economic effects of changes in the supply of money, we have simply assumed a superstructure of credit money to be erected on a foundation of gold. We now find between this superstructure and its gold foundation an intervening storey, constructed, indeed, out of credit money, which is manufactured by the central bank, but out of credit money which is only used by the other banks to form their reserves, and is not drawn upon directly by the trading community at all.

Nevertheless this does not necessitate any material alteration of the theory previously evolved. If the amount of credit money is increased, trade will be stimulated, profits and prices will rise, and more legal tender money will be drawn out. The banks will replenish their till money by drawing on the central bank. At the same time the increase in the stock of money in the country, and in the prices of commodities, will drive the rate of exchange towards the export specie point. The central bank will experience a demand for gold, both for internal circulation and for export. Both demands can be checked by a rise in the rate of interest. As has been shown in Chapter VIII, a rise in the rate of interest will tend to move the rate of exchange back from the export specie point. It will at the same time tend to produce a contraction of the central bank's loans, and this means, of course, a contraction of the deposits in the central bank, that is to say, of the reserves of the other banks. It may be that the contraction of loans is not rapid enough ; if so, it is open to the central bank itself to come into the market as a borrower, and the sums borrowed will have to be paid to it through the clearing-house by the banks at which the lenders' accounts are kept. If those banks wish to keep up their own balances at the central bank they must borrow in turn from it, and they can only borrow at the rate of interest which it chooses to ask. Thus the central bank has the power of putting pressure on the other banks to reduce their reserves, and they will then stiffen their own terms for loans. By this means the business community will be induced to curtail its borrowings, and all the consequences described in Chapters VI and IX will follow.

The responsibility for maintaining the solvency of the banking system as a whole rests almost entirely on the central bank, and the question arises, how is that bank to be guided in exercising that responsibility ? How much gold ought to be kept in reserve and how great a change in the amount of the reserve should the central bank acquiesce in before taking steps to correct it ?

This is the much-discussed gold reserve question. The solution is, of course, a matter of practical experience, upon which it would be useless to dogmatise *a priori*. The gold reserve of any country is simply a working balance. Like all working balances, however low it falls, it fulfils its function provided it is never exhausted even at the moment of greatest strain. But the moment of greatest strain cannot necessarily be recognised when it comes. In practice, therefore, a standard, more or less arbitrary, is fixed for the gold reserve (e.g. a certain proportion of the liabilities of the central bank), and steps are always taken to correct any material departure from the standard chosen. Under this system the standard reserve must be at least of such amount that if it begins to diminish it can stand whatever drain it may be subjected to in the interval before the remedial measures adopted by the central bank have become completely effective.

We have seen in Chapter IX that in an international system with a common metallic medium of exchange monetary fluctuations tend to spread themselves over the entire system. Consequently to meet internal demands the central bank can usually rely on attracting gold from abroad. The real strain on the gold reserve occurs when there is a simultaneous movement of inflation all over the world. In such a case when the banks find that they cannot supply enough gold to support the credit money which they have created, no one country will be in a position to give much help to any other. The inflation can only be reduced by means of a universal high interest rate, which will curtail loans in all countries simultaneously.

The central bank system prevails throughout Europe. It is not necessary to examine the various forms of the system in detail, but it will be useful to call attention to the salient features in one or two cases. In France (as, indeed, on the Continent generally) the use of cheques is much less common than in England, and the note-issue of the Bank of France is an important source of the creation of credit money. The liability of a bank to pay legal tender money on demand is in principle the same from the point of view of the money market, whether the credit money represented by that liability is transferable by cheque or by bank-note. But as was shown in the preceding chapters, there are some important differences. For example, the notes of the Bank of France are legal tender. Consequently they are not strictly " credit " money, i.e. though the note entitles the holder to receive coin on demand, the note itself is just as good for purposes of internal circulation as the coin. The Bank of France, however, maintains a gigantic reserve—probably a far greater reserve than would be necessary to maintain the convertibility of the notes even if they were not legal tender. And, as a matter of fact, the notes are not really convertible into *gold* at all, but into *coin*. Formerly the French coinage was bimetallic. Gold and silver circulated together, both being unlimited legal tender and both being subject to free coinage. The ratio between them for the purposes of currency corresponds closely with the ratio between the values

of the two metals in the open market. But when
the rapid depreciation of silver in terms of gold
began about forty years ago, this equilibrium was
upset. The ratio established for the French coinage
represented a serious and growing overvaluation of
silver in terms of gold and undervaluation of gold in
terms of silver. The consequent tendency for silver to
displace gold drove the French Government to suspend
the free coinage of silver altogether, in order to save
their currency from becoming one of silver only to the
entire exclusion of gold. Since then all fresh coinage
(except for small change of limited legal tender) has
been of gold ; but nevertheless the old silver five-franc
pieces, which were coined as unlimited legal tender
under the former regime, still remain unlimited legal
tender, although their intrinsic value has fallen to less
than half their nominal value. A portion of the reserve
of the Bank of France is composed of these coins, and
as its notes are convertible into coin, and not, as of
right, into *gold* coin, the Bank can always redeem its notes
if it chooses with silver five-franc pieces, which are of no
use for international purposes except within the " Latin
Union." It is not the actual practice of the Bank to
exercise this option in such a way as to drive its notes
to a discount. Indeed, the notes are circulating side by
side with gold coins, and the legal tender laws preserve
their equality. No one ever need present notes in
order to obtain gold for any purpose except export. If
in such circumstances the Bank of France cashes the
notes in silver, the demand for gold can still be met
from the gold coin in circulation. But to collect this
for export will be a task involving delay and expense.
Thus the Bank as the holder of the only reserve out of

which gold can be readily obtained in large quantities is in a position to exercise a very powerful check upon the export of gold. The result is that France is less exposed than other great commercial nations to the influence of trade fluctuations which start elsewhere. The Bank's discretion to refuse to part with its gold acts as a barrier against foreign monetary disturbances, in the same way as an inconvertible paper currency, though with less effect, since the Bank of France scrupulously maintains the parity between notes and gold.

Since the notes are legal tender and there is no hard-and-fast limit, such as is enforced in England, upon the amount issued otherwise than against gold,[1] the Bank of France must be regarded as possessing in some degree the power of creating money, not merely in the broad sense of credit money, but in the strict and narrow sense of legal tender money, which is as good as coin of the Republic. When credit money has been created and legal tender money is needed by the depositors for payment of wages and similar purposes, the Bank can supply their needs by the simple mechanism of the printing press. But if it issues legal tender notes in this way the amount of legal tender money in the country is thereby increased; there will ensue the stimulus to trade and the rise of prices by which an inflation of the currency is accompanied; and, as we have seen in Chapter IX, the rate of exchange will move towards the export specie point. In other words, France being filled up with currency, the money will tend to over-

---

[1] There is a maximum limit upon the total note-issue. But the issue does not ordinarily approach very near to this limit, and when it shows signs of doing so the limit is usually extended by amending legislation.

flow into the neighbouring countries. Of course, only
the gold can be exported, but if gold cannot be obtained the notes will ultimately fall to a discount, and
so the Bank must be prepared to part with gold as a
last resort. It can keep its gold, however, by raising
the rate of interest. By that means it will attract
loans from abroad, and so (see Chapter IX) will drive
the rate of exchange back from the export specie point.

But this measure, while attracting foreign lenders,
will discourage the domestic borrower, and so diminish
the amount of credit money. The superfluous notes
will no longer be needed for circulation, and will return
to the Bank of France in repayment of loans and cancellation of credit money. Thus so long as the parity
between notes and gold is to be maintained the action
of the Bank of France is governed by very nearly the
same principles as that of the Bank of England. The
most important difference is that, as no one can claim
gold as of right from the Bank of France, it need not
be so prompt as the Bank of England to adjust the rate
of interest, and the rate of interest is therefore less
sensitive in France than in England.

As a matter of fact, however, this is not the only
method open to a central bank or Government which
is responsible for maintaining the parity of a legal
tender note-issue. The essential condition of maintaining parity is that, in the event of a redundancy of
currency occurring, it will be possible promptly to
withdraw a sufficient portion of the notes from circulation to relieve the redundancy. The raising of the rate
of interest accomplishes this by discouraging borrowing.
The same end could be brought about by borrowing a
sum of money in the open market and cancelling the

notes received. A third method has been devised, and is in successful operation in India, Austria-Hungary, and other countries. This method is based on the fact that a redundancy or scarcity of currency in any country makes itself felt in the rates of exchange on foreign countries. The Indian currency is composed mainly of overvalued silver rupees and notes convertible only into these coins and not into gold. The Indian Government does not attempt like France to keep a gold reserve on a large scale to secure the practical convertibility and consequently the parity of the rupee. It is always receiving rupees in India, and has to make large remittances to London, where it holds a large fund of money and readily marketable securities, to meet its expenditure in England. If the rupee shows signs of depreciating, or, in other words, if the rate of exchange tends towards the point at which, if the rupee were gold, gold would be exported from India, then the Indian Government simply diminishes these remittances. The rupees which begin to accumulate in India are withheld from circulation, and its payments are made in England out of the funds held in London. If this expedient is insufficient, the Government sells bills on London in India and retains the rupees received for them. In the contrary case when the rate of exchange is approaching the import specie point, showing that there is a scarcity of currency, the exchange operations are increased, more rupees go into circulation in India, and the additional money received in London is invested, or lent out at call, and added to the fund or reserve held there. The effect of this system is that currency conditions in India tend to be an exact image of those in England, and as there is a free market for gold in England, Indian trade is subject to much the same fluctuations as if there were a free market for gold in India.

In Austria-Hungary the maintenance of the gold-value of the paper currency is less completely dependent on the regulation of the foreign exchanges in this way than in India, for there is a large gold reserve which by itself would be sufficient to secure the convertibility of the notes.

One other central banking system calls for mention, that of Germany. The enactments regulating the Reichsbank contain a special feature which was suggested by the experience of the Bank of England in financial crises after the Bank Act of 1844, under which it still works. As already explained, the Bank of England is permitted to issue notes against securities to a total value of some £18,000,000, but is compelled to hold in reserve the full value in gold of any notes issued in excess of that sum. So long as this limitation is observed the additional notes are practically gold certificates. In times of crisis, however, when more credit money had been created than the supply of legal tender money regulated on this basis would support, the Executive Government more than once gave authority to the Bank to increase the supply of legal tender money by issuing notes in contravention of the law and undertook to obtain from Parliament the necessary legislation to legalise this step. It was recognised that this was a valuable resource in the exceptional strain of a crisis, but it was open to the grave objection that it involved an illegality which could only be corrected *ex post facto*. In the constitution of the German Bank, in order to retain the advantages

of the system without this defect, it was provided that
ordinarily notes should not be issued in excess of a
fixed limit, called the " Contingent," except against
their full value in coin or bullion, but the Reichsbank
was given power to issue in excess of that limit on payment of a special tax of 5 per cent on the value of the
notes so issued. Thus it is not profitable to issue notes
in excess of the Contingent, otherwise than on a " gold
certificate " basis, unless the rate of interest exceeds
5 per cent and covers the tax. It was intended that
this arrangement should be practically automatic : that
the high rate of interest which represents a demand
for currency should itself lead the Reichsbank to issue
additional notes, which would be rapidly withdrawn
again from circulation on the demand slackening. In
practice, however, the Reichsbank finds it desirable
to exercise considerable discretion in the issue of excess
notes, and to determine its action with a view to the
public interest rather than according to immediate
profit and loss. In fact, there is a palpable fallacy in
the automatic theory, since the mere increase in the
amount of legal tender money tends to make business
more profitable and so to raise the rate of interest. A
high rate of interest may therefore mean that the
supply of money, so far from being insufficient, is growing too fast. The note-issue of the Reichsbank is
limited, apart from the regulation respecting the Contingent, to three times its reserve, and consequently
the Bank really depends like other central banks
mainly on raising the rate of interest above the " profit
rate " to check inflation.

Without stopping further to examine the many
varieties of banking institutions based on the central

bank system, it is necessary to refer briefly to the banking and currency institutions of the United States, which play a very important part in the finance of the world. The banking system of the United States is very complicated, partly because banking is a matter subject to the concurrent jurisdiction of the Federal and State legislatures, partly because the Federal law on the subject is itself very elaborate. The right of note-issue (otherwise than by the Government) is confined to the banks chartered under the Federal law, which are called "National Banks," but as the National Banks are not allowed to have branches, there are multitudes, literally thousands, of separate banks all with a right of note-issue. Nevertheless so far as the note-issue is concerned the position is not very different from that which obtains under the regime of a central bank with a monopoly of issue. The notes are subject to a Federal tax, and as the entire issue of every bank has to be covered by United States bonds deposited with the Treasury, which are forced up to an artificial price in consequence of the demand for this purpose, much of the profit goes to the Federal Government. The notes are legal tender, and their convertibility is absolutely safeguarded by stringent statutory enactments. Consequently they circulate alongside the other varieties of paper money (which they resemble somewhat in appearance) and no one ever considers whether notes which pass through his hands are bank-notes or United States notes, or gold certificates or silver certificates. From the point of view of the creation of credit money the circulation of the National Banks may be ignored, as really forming part of the currency system, not of the banking system of the country.

To turn to the banking system proper, the national banks are divided into three classes according to the places in which they are situated. New York, Chicago, and St. Louis are classed as Central Reserve Cities, and a number of other large towns are classed as Reserve Cities. A National Bank in a Central Reserve City is required to keep a reserve of legal tender money not less than 25 per cent of its deposit liabilities. A National Bank in a Reserve City is also required to keep a 25 per cent reserve. But this need not be all in cash, for it may deposit half of it with a National Bank in a Central Reserve City. And a bank in a place which is not even a Reserve City must have a 15 per cent reserve, but may deposit three-fifths of this with a bank in a Reserve City. Thus, instead of there being a central bank with which the other banks deposit their reserves, there is a group of banks in New York (and less important groups in Chicago and St. Louis) to fulfil that function. And instead of the banking in the smaller towns being undertaken by branches of the larger banks, it is in the hands of small banks which depend for assistance in emergencies on the banks in the Reserve Cities, which, in turn, depend on the New York banks. United States banking has had an unfortunate history, and the system above described has been the object of much hostile criticism. The prevalent opinion in financial circles is that a central bank ought to be established, which should definitely accept the responsibility of protecting the national stock of gold by making timely adjustments in the rate of interest. No system of statutory bank reserves can possibly be as efficient as the exercise of an expert discretion. Indeed, the statutory reserves enforced in the United States have been found to be an illusory safeguard in times of crisis. If a sudden demand for legal tender money reduces some of the reserves below the statutory limits, the banks which are placed in this position are precluded from lending any more money until they have restored themselves to a legal footing. In the last resort, no doubt, the law is broken wholesale, and broken with impunity. But even so the distribution of the reserves of cash among thousands of banks is a serious source of weakness.

Another defect in the system is that the existence of a large number of mutually independent banks is bound to lead to much imprudent banking. A large bank with many branches will take care that its local managers do not take up any unsound business. It will have an expert staff with a vast fund of banking experience, and will be anxious, above all things, not to risk its established position. A small local bank is much more likely to be led away by the attractions of speculative enterprise, and indirect control by some larger financial organisation is by no means a restraining influence. Imprudent banking is profitable, and in that simple fact lies the explanation of many financial crises.

For historical reasons the United States currency system, like the banking system, is an accumulation of picturesque survivals unillumined by any intelligible theory. A nucleus of inconvertible paper, or "greenbacks," subsequently made convertible, dates back to the time of the Civil War. Approximately contemporary with this issue is the note-issue of the National Banks. So long as the standard of value was the paper dollar, which, having been overissued, was inconvertible and at a discount, the National Bank notes were convertible into legal tender paper and practically not into metal. With the resumption of specie payments in 1878, the paper dollar reverted to its full gold value. In the interval the free coinage and even the unlimited legal tender character of the silver dollar had been abandoned, and, as in Europe, the coinage had passed on to simple gold basis. There was political opposition, however, to this change, and though the free coinage of silver was not restored, the silver dollar was again made unlimited legal tender, and a certain prescribed amount of silver was required to be coined every year. Thus after 1878 the currency included Government notes, National Bank notes, gold and silver. And, as the public were accustomed to handle paper rather than metal, the gold and silver dollars were for the most part represented for the purposes of circulation by gold certificates and silver certificates, the coins being held in reserve by the Government to the full value of the certificates issued. The annual coinages of silver continued until 1893, when the consequent inflation of the currency was found to be threatening the convertibility of the greenback into gold, and the coinage of silver remained an acute political question till 1900. Since that date, however, the currency of the United States has been placed definitely on a gold basis, and the obligation of converting all paper, including silver certificates, into gold on demand has been placed on the Treasury. Since new greenbacks are not issued, while silver is only coined for the purposes of a subsidiary currency and the circulation of the National Banks is limited by their holdings of United States bonds, the elasticity of the currency is really provided

for only by the coinage of gold or the issue of gold certificates on the deposit of gold bullion. With all its
complications the United States currency does not at
the present time differ very much from the system in
force in England, except that the volume of notes against
which no gold is held, including $200,000,000 out of
the $350,000,000 of greenbacks, and practically all
the National Bank circulation and silver certificates,
is enormously greater and is not absolutely fixed in
amount.

XIV

THE last two chapters have been chiefly taken up with facts. The review of these facts is a necessary preliminary to the transfer of our investigation from a hypothetical to the actual world. For though we have demonstrated that, with the assumptions made, the consequences of a monetary disturbance exhibit a remarkable correspondence with the known characteristics of a trade fluctuation, it is only when all artificial assumptions are abandoned and the argument is applied to actual conditions that this correspondence can acquire the force of an inductive proof.

In the present and two following chapters I propose to describe how fluctuations actually occur. In all the cases dealt with in Chapters V, VI, VIII, and IX a sudden isolated contraction or expansion of the currency was assumed to supervene upon a perfectly stable economic condition, and the effects of the disturbance were followed out up to the attainment of a new state of equilibrium under the altered conditions. But in practice the influences which produce fluctuations are not sudden, but gradual ; they are continuous, not discontinuous. Nor can we postulate an initial condition of stability. Trade is never normal ; in times of average prosperity it is always on either the upward or the downward path ; when it ceases to improve it is on the verge of collapse, when it ceases to slacken it is beginning to recover. But in order to trace the history of a fluctuation it is necessary to begin somewhere, and perhaps the best stage to take as a beginning is the moment at which a state of inflation collapses, and a period of declining trade is entered upon. At such a time the hasty and even panic-stricken efforts of the bankers to restrain the creation of credit money, and so to return to a position of safety, approximate very closely to the discontinuous disturbances which we have already studied.

Suppose, then, that a state of inflation exists. It need not be assumed to exist everywhere, nor yet need it be confined to one country. It may exist in a more or less pronounced degree in several countries, while others may be almost entirely free from the taint. It must next be supposed that something occurs to make the banking community reconsider their position in one of the countries where there is inflation, that is to say, where the amount of credit money has outstripped the prudent proportion to the supply of legal tender money. This occurrence would probably take the form of a signal of distress from one of the weaker banks. Such a bank, having been tempted by the high profits which accompany the process of inflation to lend too freely, will have found that some of the enterprises to which it has been lending need more money to carry them through than it can provide out of its own resources. The natural course is to borrow from its neighbours. At a time when they have a margin of cash over and above the reserves they think necessary they will lend readily. But we are supposing that a state of inflation already exists, so that they

will have no such margin. They can only afford to lend
if the rate of interest is put up. By that measure they
can reduce the inflation and attract gold from abroad.
But of foreign countries some are likewise suffering
from inflated credit money and the others presumably
have not gold actually to spare. They must all raise
their rates of interest to protect their gold and so the
process of reducing inflation begins. This raising of the
rate of interest amounts practically to an intimation
to all the banks which have been sailing near the wind
that they cannot count on being able to borrow readily
in an emergency. From this point there starts a sys-
tematic endeavour of the banks in all the centres of
inflation to reduce credit money. Except that there
are many such centres, the resulting phenomena correspond very closely with those which were shown in
Chapter IX to follow from an arbitrary contraction of
the currency in one country. The tendency of gold to
flow from all quarters towards the centres of disturbance
until their shortage of money is made up at the expense
of the rest of the world has already been described in
that chapter. The gold is attracted partly by the
actual shortage which itself moves the rate of exchange
toward the import specie point (as was made clear in
the example of the cisterns in Chapter IX), partly by
the high rate of interest. The former is really the more
potent influence of the two. The high rate of interest is
essentially a temporary condition, for it is not only
attracting gold from abroad, but is at the same time
discouraging the creation of credit money. When the
excess of credit money has been relieved the rate of
interest will revert of course to the profit rate, but
equilibrium cannot be completely restored until the

shortage of money has been made up. The difference of level in the cisterns must be reduced until the difference of pressure is no longer sufficient to keep the valves open. Further, the effectiveness of the high rate of interest in attracting gold must not be exaggerated. It is rare for a difference as great as 3 per cent to exist between the rates prevailing in two great financial centres. But even a difference of 3 per cent over a period of two months would only cover a loss by exchange of $\frac{1}{2}$ per cent on the capital involved.

For example, suppose that the rate of interest for two months bills is 3 per cent per annum in London and 6 per cent in New York. If the rate of exchange for telegraphic transfers were at par—say, $4·86$\frac{1}{2}$ to £1— then a man with £10,000 to his credit in London which he wants to lend for two months could obtain in place of that sum $48,650 in New York. If he lends it in London he will get interest to the amount of £50, being 3 per cent per annum for two months on £10,000. If he obtains the dollars to lend in New York he will receive $486·50 as interest, and if the rate of exchange is still at par he can get back the £10,000 for his capital and £100 instead of £50 for his interest. But if, apart from the influence of the high rate of interest at New York, the rate of exchange would be at par (i.e. if the English cistern and the United States cistern are both full up to the same level), then the actual rate of exchange will be displaced from parity by that influence. So considerable a difference in the rate of interest cannot continue indefinitely. Assume that it is not expected to continue beyond two months, and that for some time afterwards the rate of interest in London and New York alike is expected to be 3 per cent. These expectations will be reflected in the rates for other bills, which should be approximately as follows :—

	London	New York
Two months	3 per cent	.. 6 per cent
Three months	3 per cent	.. 5 per cent
Four months	3 per cent	.. 4½ per cent
Six months	3 per cent	.. 4 per cent

With these rates the actual difference of interest on £10,000 would be precisely £50, whether it is lent for two, three, four, or six months.

This difference would just be counteracted by an adjustment of ½ per cent in the rate of exchange. If the rate of exchange were 4·84 at the beginning of the period, it would be expected to rise to par or 4·86½ at the end of two months, along with the drop expected to occur at that time in the rate of interest in New York. The following table compares the net result of lending £10,000 in London or New York :—

	Interest on £10,000 in London	Interest on $48,400 in New York	Interest and Principal in New York	Equivalent in London at 4·86½	Net profit
2 months ...	£50 ...	$484 ...	$48,884 ...	£10,048 2s. ...	£48 2s.
3 months ...	£75 ...	$605 ...	$49,005 ...	£10,073 ...	£73
4 months ...	£100 ...	$726 ...	$49,126 ...	£10,097 17s. ...	£97 17s.
6 months ...	£150 ...	$968 ...	$49,368 ...	£10,147 11s. ...	£147 11s.

Thus it is just not worth while to lend in New York in spite of the 6 per cent obtainable there, and the rate of exchange of 4·84, as a matter of fact, would barely be low enough to attract gold. It is clear, then, that in order to bring in gold a high rate of interest must be fairly prolonged. In practice the great central banks know when they are short of gold, and instead of relying on the rate of interest to attract it, they often arrange privately with one another for such movements of gold as appear expedient. It is sometimes found that gold is sent to a place where the exchanges are still far from the specie point, or, to return to our illustration of the cisterns, it is sometimes convenient to transfer water in a bucket instead of awaiting the automatic action of the valves. This is particularly the case with the Bank of France, which can defend its gold from attack under a rampart of overvalued five-franc pieces, but which is unwilling to push its use of this defence so far as to drive its notes to a discount. But quite apart from this resource it can choose its own moment for sending gold to London, which is the entrepôt for supplying the needs of the world, and the knowledge that it will do so prevents other people from speculating in the export of gold. If the Paris exchange on London goes up to the export specie point, any one in Paris who has a considerable quantity of gold can send it to London without loss, but if the Bank of France is also going to send gold, the exchanges may have gone back to par in a few days. In that case it would have been more advantageous to wait and save the cost of freight by using the machinery of the exchange. This advantage in controlling gold movements is open to any central bank which possesses the only large stock of gold to be found in the country in which it is situated, and consequently in practice the theory of the specie points is often found to be quite at fault.

In the case of India and other countries where, as explained in the last chapter, the gold value of the currency is maintained by a regulation of the foreign exchanges, there will be no export or import of gold,

but there will be a contraction of the currency or of
credit money or both, in sympathy with the contraction occurring in the gold-using countries. It
should be observed that under the Indian system an
excessive creation of credit money in comparison with
the amount of currency in circulation will tend to
depreciate the exchange value of the rupee and to
occasion a withdrawal of rupees from circulation in the
manner described in the last chapter (page 167). The
rate of exchange depends on the total supply of money
including credit money, and not on the supply of legal
tender money or currency only. Again, if, as we are
now supposing, steps are taken in Europe to reduce
the amount of credit money, and the consequent rise in
the value of gold necessitates a withdrawal of rupees,
the proportion of rupees to credit money in India will
be diminished and the amount of credit money will have
to be reduced by an increase in the rate of interest
there also.

Of all these various proceedings London is the centre.
In a time of emergency (and indeed at all times) it is
desirable that the business of distributing the supply
of gold be centralised, and the centre relied on for this
purpose is London. For this choice there are several
reasons, historical and geographical, but perhaps the
most important qualification of London for the purpose
is to be found in the practice of the Bank of England to
maintain a " free " market for gold. The Bank undertakes to honour all demands upon it in gold, and gold
flows in without restraint because every one knows that
it will flow out again without stint. Nothing deters
people so much from entrusting money or anything
else to any agency or institution as the fear that they

cannot freely get it back again when they want it. Thus the Bank of England can collect any amount of gold at any time by merely offering a high price for it in the form of a high rate of interest.

Until, then, the shortage of money which we have supposed to have occurred is made up, gold will flow from all over the world (probably through London) to the points of shortage. Presently the exchanges will show the effect of the movement of gold; it will cease to be profitable to send it from most countries. But though the stream of gold is no longer in spate there will still remain the usual flow from the gold-mining countries, and that flow will be directed to the countries where the shortage of currency occurred so long as the rates of exchange differ materially from parity.

From the time when the rise in the rate of interest occurred the phenomena already shown to be character-istic of a depression will have appeared. As the shortage of money comes to be distributed over the whole gold-using world, the restriction of business, the contraction of profits, the diminution of employment, and the fall of prices are similarly distributed.

There is no need to repeat here the description of these processes which has already been given in Chapters VI and IX. We are now concerned not with the direct consequences of a given monetary disturbance, but with the influences at work to modify and, perhaps in the end, to counteract those consequences. In particular are we to regard the tendency towards renewed inflation which experience teaches us to expect after a period of depression as a fortuitous disturbance which may come sooner or later, or as a reaction the seeds of which are already sown ? To put the same problem in another form, when the position of equilibrium which should follow a disturbance according to the theory in Chapter VI is attained, is there any reason, apart from visible causes of renewed disturbance, why that equilibrium should not continue ? It is very commonly held that the causes of the further departure from the equilibrium position, which experience leads us to expect, are psychological. The recovery of equilibrium after depression is a process which might be expected to encourage optimism, and it is easy to say that, once a state of optimism has been engendered, *l'appétit vient en mangeant*, every one will grow more confident as he learns his neighbours' confidence, and the general expectation of prosperity will lead on to another period of inflation.

This view is not without plausibility, and no doubt there is a quality of human nature which makes hope and fear contagious, and which may be as potent in a market as in an army. At the same time trade movements are characterised by an inflexible persistence which calls for some deeper explanation than this. A revival of trade will pursue its way undeterred through obstacles which might well be expected to dissipate every vestige of optimism which may have helped it on its way. Strikes, wars, bad harvests, and earthquakes seem powerless to interfere with its even progress, or, at any rate, to do more than interrupt it for a moment. It survives false alarms of collapse no less than substantial calamities. Then, often almost without warning, a turning-point is reached and it is found that the ebb of trade, like its flow, cannot be stopped and ean hardly be hastened or impeded. If the causes of fluctuations were merely, or even chiefly, psychological this would be impossible.

And we have already seen some forces at work which will help to explain them otherwise. We are supposing that the sequence of events described in Chapter VI is occurring practically throughout the world. The gold movements which formed the subject of Chapter IX are completed ; the plethora of credit money has been relieved ; the reserves of the banks have been restored. There remains the final stage in which there will be no further reduction in the stock of credit money, but the full output of industry will gradually be resumed as wages and prices fall. This at least is what we ended with in Chapter VI. And no doubt, having started with the wholly chimerical assumption of a community continuing indefinitely in perfect economic equilibrium, it was legitimate to assume that, after the necessary adjustments called for by a disturbance of equilibrium have been completed, the banks would be able to regain an economic equilibrium as placid and unruffled as before. But now we have abandoned all such artificial assumptions, and we must face the practical difficulties which will lie in the way of an establishment of stable conditions.

It will be remembered that the portion of the economic organisation of Society which is most sensitive to changes in the rate of interest is the class of dealers, both wholesale and retail. The business of a producer usually requires a large amount of plant or fixed capital. The fixed capital is set up in the expectation that the profit of the business will yield a reasonable rate of interest upon it ; but, once it has been set up, it will be better to keep it at work so long as there is *any*

profit over and above working expenses, than to leave
it idle and earning nothing. Producers are therefore
willing to meet a shrinkage of price or an increase of
working expenses out of profits in preference to restricting their output, and they are very slow to
respond to so slight an increase of their aggregate
expenses as is involved in a rise in the rate of interest
on temporary loans.

A dealer, on the other hand, keeps stocks on hand on
grounds of convenience. A man who keeps on an
average £10,000 worth of goods on his premises is
paying (or losing) a substantial sum in interest—if the
rate of interest is 3 per cent and if he has borrowed the
entire £10,000 from his bankers he is paying at the rate
of £300 a year or nearly £1 a day. This he will only be
willing to do if the convenience of having this quantity
and variety of goods at call is worth £1 a day. If the
rate of interest goes up to 6 per cent, he will have to
reconsider the question of what stocks it is worth while
to keep. Rather than pay £2 a day he will make some
small sacrifice of convenience, and will delay the replenishment of his stocks. The effects of the action
which the dealers are so induced to take we traced in
Chapter VI—the curtailment of orders, the restriction
of output, the contraction of credit money, the drop in
demand, the decline of prices, and the decrease of
employment. And among these various effects we
showed that falling prices are associated with a low
profit rate. On completing the adjustment of credit
money to reserves the bankers will let the rate of
interest revert to equality with the profit rate. Now
to the dealer the cost of maintaining stocks is represented not by the natural rate of interest, but by the

profit rate. He loses in exactly the same way by a fall in the value of the goods, while he is holding them, as by the charge made by his banker for interest. If he expects prices to fall he will try to reduce his stocks in precisely the same way as if he had to pay extra interest.

It is in order to counteract the effect of the falling prices that the bankers fix a rate of interest lower than the natural rate by the rate at which prices are believed to be falling. If they fail to do this they will find their business gradually falling off and superfluous stocks of gold accumulating in their vaults. Here we may digress for a moment to consider a special case. What if the rate of depreciation of prices is actually *greater* than the natural rate of interest ? If that is so nothing that the bankers can do will make borrowing sufficiently attractive. Business will be revolving in a vicious circle ; the dealers unwilling to buy in a falling market, the manufacturers unable to maintain their output in face of ever-diminishing orders, dealers and manufacturers alike cutting down their borrowings in proportion to the decline of business, demand falling in proportion to the shrinkage in credit money, and with the falling demand, the dealers more unwilling to buy than ever. This, which may be called " stagnation " of trade, is of course exceptional, but it deserves our attention in passing.

From the apparent impasse there is one way out—a drastic reduction of money wages. If at any time this step is taken the spell will be broken. Wholesale prices will fall abruptly, the *expectation* of a further fall will cease, dealers will begin to replenish their stocks, manufacturers to increase their output, dealers and manufacturers alike will borrow again, and the stock of credit money will grow. In fact the profit rate will recover, and will again equal or indeed exceed the natural rate. The market rate, however, will be kept *below* the profit rate, since in the preceding period of stagnation the bankers' reserves will have been swollen beyond the necessary proportions, and the bankers will desire to develop their loan and discount business.

It should be observed that this phenomenon of stagnation will only be possible where the *expected* rate of depreciation of the prices of commodities happens to be high. As to the precise circumstances in which this will be so, it is difficult to arrive at any very definite conclusion. Dealers will be guided partly by the tendency of prices in the immediate past, partly by the state of demand at existing prices, partly by what they know of the conditions of production.

A remarkable example of trade stagnation occurred at the end of the period from 1873 to 1897, when there had been a prolonged falling off in the gold supply, and in consequence a continuous fall in prices. The rate of interest in London throughout a period of no less than seven years, ending with 1897, averaged only $1\frac{1}{2}$ per cent, and yet superfluous gold went on accumulating in the vaults of the Bank of England.

It is clear that, if this special phenomenon of stagnation occurs, the moment when recovery begins will find the banks eager to attract borrowers to relieve them of their large superfluous stocks of gold. In that case there is no doubt of a period of activity following, since there is room for a large increase in the supply of credit money.

We are more concerned, however, with the normal

case, where the banks never lose the power of stimulating borrowing and where depression is therefore
never exaggerated to the point of stagnation. To the
question whether in that normal case there is a
tendency for inflation to succeed to depression and
depression to inflation, we will pass in the next chapter.

XV

THE GENESIS OF A FLUCTUATION—*continued*

In Chapter VII it was mentioned that when the volume of credit money is increased or diminished by the banks the corresponding increase or decrease in the cash in circulation does not occur immediately, but only after a perceptible interval. We are now supposing that the banks have found it necessary to curtail credit money, and that the consequent contraction of effective demand for commodities has led to the inevitable restriction of output. It will be remembered that, rather than let their plant lie idle, manufacturers will sacrifice part or even the whole of their profits, and that in this way the restriction of output is mitigated. If all producers insisted on stopping work unless they could obtain a normal rate of profit, there would be a greater restriction of output and more workmen would be discharged, and in that case the proceeds of the diminished output would be divided (approximately) in the same proportion between the capitalists and the workmen as before. But in consequence of the sacrifice of profits to output which actually occurs, the number of workmen in employment and therefore also the aggregate of working-class earnings will not be so severely diminished as they would otherwise be. Thus the capitalists will get a smaller proportion and the workmen a greater proportion of the gross proceeds than before. But anything which tends to increase or maintain working-class earnings tends to increase or maintain the amount of cash in the hands of the working classes. If the banks have succeeded in reducing the outstanding amount of credit money by 10 per cent, they will probably have reduced the incomes of the people with banking accounts by 10 per cent, but the earnings of the working classes will have been reduced in a much smaller proportion—say, 5 per cent. And the cash remaining in the hands of the working classes will probably have been diminished in even a slighter degree, since a diminution of earnings will only affect a working man's accumulations of money gradually.

At the stage, therefore, at which the banks become satisfied with their position and no longer think it necessary to curtail loans or maintain a high rate of interest, a greater proportion of the available stock of legal tender money will be in circulation and a smaller proportion will be accumulated in the hands of the banks than under normal conditions. And so long as money wages are resisting reduction and encroaching on profits, this will be the case. No doubt, as money wages fall, not only will profits rise, but employment will improve, and to some extent the fall in earnings will be counteracted by this latter cause. But as business approaches normal conditions there must be a tendency on the whole for profits to recover at the expense of earnings, and cash will come back from circulation into the hands of the banks.

Here is a process at work which is likely enough to produce fluctuations. For the bankers will thereupon be ready to *increase* the stock of credit money again, and once they have embarked on this course they may find it very difficult to stop short of a dangerous inflation. In fact, in order to steer business back into stable conditions they would have to foresee the diminution of cash requirements, and to ease off the rate of interest with gradations so nicely calculated as just to effect the requisite reduction of credit money at the very final stage, when the cash requirements have also reached the normal proportion. In practice it would be impossible to know accurately even in an isolated community, still less in the world as it is, what cash requirements to anticipate or what ultimate volume of credit money to aim at. During the progress of a depression no man can say how far off the turning-point may be. And as the bankers are thus working in the dark they must be assumed to adjust their action to the facts within their cognisance, that is to say, to the state of their own assets and liabilities.

Instead of ending up, therefore, with the establish-ment of a golden mean of prosperity, unbroken by any deviation towards less or more, the depression will be marked in its later stages by a new complication. At the time when the reduction of wages is beginning to be accompanied not merely by an increase of employment, but also by an increase of profits, the banks will find that cash is beginning to accumulate in their vaults. They will ease off the rate of interest to something a little below the profit rate, and dealers will take advantage of the low rate to add to their stocks. The manufacturers will become aware of an increase in orders, and they will find that they can occupy their plant more fully. And now that stocks and output are both increased, borrowing will be increased and the bankers will have gained their end. But then the new accession to the amount of credit money means a corresponding increase of purchasing power. At existing prices the dealers find that their stocks are being depleted by the growing demand from the consumer. The prospect of rising prices is an inducement to add to their stocks as much as they can at existing prices, and so their orders to the manufacturers grow still more. As their demands on the manufacturers grow, wholesale prices go up ; and as the consumers' demands on the dealers' stocks grow, retail prices go up; and as prices go up, the money needed to finance a given quantity of goods grows greater and greater, and both dealers and manufacturers borrow more and more from their bankers. In fact here are all the characteristics of a period of trade expansion in full swing. The profit rate, of course, will have become high as soon as the downward tendency of prices was replaced by an upward tendency. Now wages do not respond quickly to economic changes, and until wages begin to rise, though increased employment means increased earnings, the demands on the banks for cash will increase but slightly. So long as the volume of credit money remains in any degree less than the reserves of cash would in the bankers' opinion justify, the rate of interest will be fixed at something short of the profit rate. As the profit rate is high, the rate of interest may according to ordinary standards appear high, but for the purpose of its effect on borrowing it is really low.

The extent and duration of the trade expansion will depend partly upon the bankers' opinion as to the volume of credit money they may prudently create. If they aimed strictly at a fixed proportion of cash to credit money, they would put up the rate of interest again as soon as that proportion was reached. But in practice the point of view of the bankers is somewhat different from this. Under any modern system of banking, whether there is a single central bank or not, and whether it is the practice to establish branch banks or not, the outlying banks are always more or less dependent on the banks in the great financial centres. The great majority of the banks will always deposit a portion of their cash with the one or several large banks, which will thus become really responsible for the national gold reserve. This the outlying banks will do partly in order that they may have the privilege of customers, and be able not merely to draw out their money, but to borrow from the central banks in an mergency, partly for the purposes of the clearing-house system. For example, in the English hierarchy of banks there rank immediately below the Bank of England, the London Clearing-house Banks, less than twenty in number, through which all cheques are settled. The country banks keep balances with these Clearing-house Banks to meet the liabilities which they will have to discharge through the Clearing-house whenever the daily balance is against them. The Clearing-house Banks themselves keep balances at the Bank of England in order to settle their mutual liabilities.

The banks really determine the amount of their " cash in hand and at the Bank of England " according to their own practical daily needs. All these sums are " working balances," held for one purpose or another. Cash is kept at a country branch bank to pay over the counter when its local customers want to draw money out. The same coins may circulate backwards and forwards in a regular eddy in one district ; part is drawn out at the end of every week to pay wages and percolates back through the shops to the banks; another part is used to supply the well-to-do with ready money and this also comes back, though perhaps not quite so quickly as the money paid in wages. Now and then the needs of the locality will vary, either through changes in local conditions or through the local effects of changes of wider scope. Perhaps the weekly wages bill will fall and part of the money previously drawn out for the payment of wages will be left week after week unused at the bank; or perhaps the weekly wages bill will rise and the banker finds that he has to pay out more cash and begins to feel anxious as to whether he will have enough to meet casual and unforeseen demands before it comes back to him. In the former case he will pack up the super-fluous specie and send it to his head office in London; in the latter case he will ask his head office to send him more. That head office will keep a reserve of cash on hand to meet demands of this kind as well as the demands of London customers; when this reserve grows beyond what is required the superfluous balance is handed over to the Bank of England; if it is depleted it is replenished by drawing on the Bank of England. Thus as the earnings of labour decline under the influence of trade depression, part of the cash which has previously been circulating between the banks and the workmen's pockets throughout the country is set free, and goes to swell the cash holdings of the Bank of England. The Bank of England regulates its reserve so as to be a prudent proportion of its liabilities, and is prepared to build up the appropriate proportion of credit money on the cash which it so receives. But the other banks regulate their cash holdings on the working balance principle, and, so long as the actual cash demands throughout the country do not increase, they will not limit their lending operations by observing any assigned proportion between cash and credit money.

Nevertheless, this does not mean that they will recognise no limitation at all to the expansion of credit money. For any increase in credit money, so far as it does not lead to an increase in cash transactions, will lead to a proportional increase in Clearing-house transactions, which will have to be supported by correspondingly larger balances at the Bank of England. A man only borrows from his banker if he wants to use the money. He uses it by paying it away and if he does not pay it away in cash he will pay it away by cheque. Thus *both* portions of the item " cash in hand and at the Bank of England," which represents the reserve in the accounts of a Joint Stock Bank, are regulated as working balances, the cash in hand being the working balance for the ready money transactions across the counter, and the " cash " (i.e. balance on current account) at the Bank of England being the working balance for the credit money transactions through the Clearing-house. The total credit money created by the banks will be so limited by them as not to outstrip the capacities of these working balances, while the Bank of England will not allow the balances to grow out of proportion to its own cash holdings. It is indeed almost, though not quite, true to say that the entire stock of credit money in England is built up not on the cash holdings of the banks taken as a whole, but on the Reserve of the Bank of England. And as the legal tender money in circulation is something like four times the average amount of the reserve, it is obvious that a small proportional change in the quantity in circulation will produce a relatively large proportional change in the reserve, and therefore in the stock of credit money. The Bank of England does not maintain blindly a fixed proportion between reserve and deposits, so that a given change in the reserve is not reflected immediately in the stock of credit money, but of course when there is a marked increase in the reserve there is a tendency towards a marked increase in the deposits and through the other banks towards a general increase in credit money. If the money in circulation is £100,000,000 and the reserve of the Bank of England is £25,000,000, then a decrease of 5 per cent or £5,000,000 in the former would raise the latter to £30,000,000, an increase of 20 per cent. If the net amount of credit money (i.e. deposits *less* cash holdings) in the other banks is £750,000,000, that might on a strictly proportional basis be raised to £900,000,000. But in practice so great an increase would not be made. Indeed, if the Bank aimed at this proportion a foreign demand for gold would spring up long before it was reached.

The banking systems of the Continent of Europe are based to a much less extent than our own on credit money. Their banking deposits are less in proportion either to wealth or population, and their stocks of legal tender money (including convertible legal tender notes) are much greater. Consequently, though the tendency which has just been described will operate on the Continent it will be less potent there than in England.

In the United States, on the other hand, the use of credit money is fully as much developed as in this

country.   Cash requirements there are complicated,
however, by the statutory reserve requirements which
have already been referred to in Chapter XII.   It might
be supposed that if a bank is compelled by law to keep
a certain proportion of its deposits in specie, it cannot
treat its cash holdings on the "working balance"
principle.   Up to a certain point this is true.   But in
practice the banks regulate their *surplus* reserves (i.e.
the excess at any time over the legal minimum) as
working balances.   Nevertheless, the system of statutory reserves does limit the creation of credit money at
the stage which we are considering, inasmuch as the
aggregate of the statutory reserves represents a much
greater proportion of the legal tender money in the
country than does the Bank of England reserve in
England.   The transfer of a given sum from circulation
to reserves in the United States should have less effect
therefore than in England in stimulating the creation
of credit money.   And no doubt this would be so, but
that, there being multitudes of independent banks large
and small in the United States with no central responsibility for banking policy, the creation of credit money is
likely to expand almost automatically in proportion to
the increase in reserves.   Sound banking *cannot* be
established by rules and formulas prescribed by law ;
without some responsible authority to exercise dis-
cretionary power, vagaries such as have been characteristic of the United States Money Market for many years
past are absolutely inevitable.   Even with a central
bank it is difficult to take precautions in time, but
centralisation, even if not a sufficient condition, is at
any rate a necessary condition of sound policy.

It is clear, then, that at the latter end of a period of

depression there is an inherent tendency towards
renewed inflation. The creation of credit money will
proceed on the basis of the visible cash requirements of
trade. But the cash requirements will ultimately grow
in proportion to the creation of credit money, and will
outstrip the available supply of gold. The rising prices
of commodities mean not only swollen profits for the
dealer, the manufacturer, and the banker, but an
increase in the cost of living to the workman. The
unhappy workman spends his life indeed between the
upper and the nether millstone ; when trade is on the
downward path he is beset with the evils of unemployment, from which he can only escape by accepting lower
wages, and when trade recovers he finds the purchasing
power of his wages still further reduced by the high
prices of commodities. It must be remembered that
over and above the extra gains made in business
through the *rising* prices and consequently high profit
rate, there are further gains made through the *high*
prices so long as the rise of wages lags behind the rise of
prices. If a manufacturer has an output of £10,000 a
month and his expenses include £4000 for raw material
and £4000 for wages, and if the prices of commodities
are rising continuously at the rate of 6 per cent per
annum, or $\frac{1}{2}$ per cent per month, then in a month's time
his bill for raw material will have risen to £4020 and his
gross receipts to £10,050, in a year's time they will
have risen to £4240 and £10,600 respectively. But
unless his workmen can insist effectively on an increase
of wages, his wages bill will remain at £4000 only.
He can afford to borrow for the purchase of raw
material at a rate of interest 6 per cent higher than
before, while his net receipts of £2000 are swollen not

only by the extra £120, which represents the general increase of money values and is not a real increase of wealth at all, but by a further sum of £240 which ought by rights to go to his workmen. That is to say, this £240 represents the amount which the workmen are losing through the change in the value of the unit in which their wages are reckoned and which under theoretic conditions of perfectly free competition without economic " friction " they would be getting.

As soon as the workmen become alive to these facts they are in a favourable position for obtaining the rise of wages to which the conditions of business entitle them. Production having been stimulated to great activity there is a scarcity of labour, or at any rate of properly trained and competent labour, and employers are so anxious to get the benefit of the high profits that they are more ready than usual to make concessions in preference to facing strikes which would leave their works idle. There follows a period of full employment and rising wages. But this means growing cash requirements, and sooner or later the banks must take action to prevent their reserves being depleted. If they act in time they may manage to relieve the inflation of credit money gradually and an actual financial crisis may be avoided. But in either case there must ensue a period of slack trade. Here, therefore, we have proved that there is an inherent tendency towards fluctuations in the banking institutions which prevail in the world as it is. But fluctuations generated in this way might be mild compared to those which actually occur, and we have already noticed some causes which are likely to aggravate them.

One of these causes is that, at the critical moment

when the banks decide that the foundation of cash is insufficient to support the existing structure of credit money, if they fail to raise the rate of interest high enough to surpass the inflated profit rate, the tendency to inflation will only be abated, not counteracted, and after a pause, will reappear with ever-accumulating force. It is difficult to say at such times what rate of interest will be just effective and not excessive, and if it is excessive it may of itself cause all the ill effects of a crisis.

It should be noted especially that at a time of expanding trade the growing demand rapidly depletes the dealers' stocks. They defend their stocks, of course, by raising retail prices and try to replenish them by giving fresh orders to the manufacturers. But when all the resources of the country are very fully employed there may be delay in executing the orders and the stocks will not be so fully replenished as the dealers intended. In that case the dealers borrow less money and the increase in the stock of credit money is so far retarded. The banks may then recover control, but as the check in the creation of purchasing power will diminish demand again, the dealers' stocks will begin to increase and they will again increase their borrowings. In that case the banks would find that they had lost control again, and thus they might drift into a very precarious position.

Another cause which tends to aggravate trade fluctuations is that imprudent banking is profitable. In a period of buoyant trade such as marks the recovery from a state of depression the profit rate is high, and the rate of interest received by the banks on their loans and discounts is correspondingly high. It may be that during the depression the banks have had to be content with 1 or 1½ per cent. When the recovery begins they find in quite a short time that they can earn 4 or 5 per cent. This is not 4 or 5 per cent on their own capital, but on the money which they lend, which may be five or ten times their capital. That portion of their deposits which is represented by cash in hand is idle and earns nothing, and they are eager to swell their profits by reducing their cash and reserves and increasing their loans and discounts. Working balances are more or less elastic and can at a pinch be reduced, but the lower its reserves fall the more likely is the bank to find it necessary to borrow from other institutions. Again, the readier a bank is to lend, the more likely it is to lend to speculative enterprises, the more likely it is to suffer losses through the total or perhaps temporary failure of such enterprises, and the more likely it is to show a balance on the wrong side of its accounts when it needs to borrow. When many banks have yielded to these temptations a crisis is almost inevitable, or if an acute crisis with its accompaniment of widespread bankruptcies is avoided, there is bound to be a very severe and probably prolonged depression during which the top-heavy structure of credit money is gently pulled down brick by brick.

This evil of over-speculation is one to which the United States with its 20,000 separate banks, large and small, is peculiarly subject. Not only has the small banker less sense of responsibility than the large, but he is often more interested in some other business than in banking, and uses the bank to forward the interests of that other business. He may be engaged in business which is in its nature speculative and risky, and will light-heartedly involve the bank in the same risks in order to make the most of the opportunities afforded by good trade.

It will probably be only a minority of the banks that overreach themselves in speculation, and it may not occur in all countries. But the prudent banks have no means of guarding themselves against the consequences of their neighbours' rashness. They could hardly be expected to increase their reserves beyond what they believe to be a prudent proportion. It is true that a central bank, in those countries where such an institution exists, can take this precaution. But it will only do so if aware of the over-speculation. Of this, however, it will have no accurate or complete knowledge, and it will experience great difficulty in determining what measures are to be taken.

If over-speculation begins in one country it quickly aggravates the inflation not only there, but in all other countries. For the rates of exchange on other countries are pushed up to export specie point, gold is sent to them, and their banks proceed to lend more freely and add to the stock of credit money.

In fact, all through the progress of a fluctuation there will be constant international adjustments of this kind. Not only do the forces which cause and influence fluctuations work with varying rapidity and intensity in different countries, but minor and transitory fluctuations are being caused here and there by disturbances of demand and supply such as were described in Chapter X. Each country is to some extent guarded from the influences of its neighbours, since its stock of money may oscillate within the limits imposed by the specie points of the rate of exchange without leading to any direct movement of gold. But the tendency of the gold which flows out of the gold-mining countries to go to the places where the rate of exchange is most favourable to it is always equalising monetary conditions throughout the world.

XVI

FINANCIAL CRISES

At the end of the last chapter we had brought the history of a fluctuation through the period of greatest depression and the subsequent recovery right up to a renewed state of inflation, and we showed that in this latter state there might be present many of the factors which are likely to produce a financial crisis. A financial crisis is so frequent an accompaniment of the transition from inflation to depression that some examination of its causes and characteristics is necessary to a complete understanding of trade fluctuations. It is not easy to say precisely what constitutes a financial crisis, but broadly it may be defined to be an escape from inflation by way of widespread failures and bankruptcies instead of by a gradual reduction of credit money.

Now the function of the credit of both banks and borrowers in the creation of credit money was explained in Chapter VII. In some cases the assets of a bank, so far as represented by loans to traders, are secured by bills bearing the names both of the dealers who gave and of the manufacturers who received the orders on the completion of which the loans will mature, and the bank would only suffer loss if both the parties to the transaction failed. In other cases the borrowers' assets alone are pledged and if they fail the money is lost. It is obvious that the risk of failure must vary widely with different forms of business. Some trades are much more affected by fluctuations than others. When the consumer finds his purchasing power diminished he will not economise his expenditure equally in all directions. Here the distinction between " elastic " and " inelastic " demand will apply ; he will sacrifice more of his expenditure on articles of which the demand is elastic than on those of which the demand is inelastic. In other words, luxuries will be more affected than comforts, and comforts more than necessaries. The effects upon production as a whole will be those which have been described, but will be very unequally distributed among the several industries. Agriculture, for example, will be hardly touched. The stocks of cereals are not subject to immediate variation, since they are replenished by the natural growth of the crops. The market for meat is no doubt affected both because the supply is subject to more direct control and because the demand for meat is more elastic than the demand for bread. But, nevertheless, for agriculture trade depressions are hardly a question of urgent practical moment. With regard to manufactures the demand is nearly always elastic. Some manufactured articles are necessaries, for example, clothes. But even in the case of clothes the quality varies so infinitely that the demand is for all practical purposes very elastic. And on the whole more manufactured articles are to be classed as comforts or luxuries than as necessaries.

There is one all-important class of industry which demands more detailed consideration ; that is the production of fixed capital. In this class are included the building and shipbuilding trades, the construction of roads and railways, and to a great extent the manufacture of machinery and vehicles. It follows that the same class also covers the greater part of the iron and steel trades, and brick-making and quarrying.

These industries really depend ultimately for the demand for their products upon the rate at which savings are accumulating. Far the greater part of the savings of any community come from the well-to-do. However thrifty the working classes may be, the available margin on their wages is small compared with the available margin on the incomes of the rich. And as the effects of a trade depression are felt first by profits, there will probably be an early slackening in saving. It is very difficult for a man whose income is suddenly diminished to economise on his personal expenditure. Economies can only be adopted gradually, and until they are adopted the loss of income is met by a curtailment of saving. For this reason the industries engaged in the production of fixed capital are peculiarly sensitive to fluctuations in the general state of trade. The effective demand for fixed capital is very high when trade is good and very low when trade is bad, and the consequences are to be seen both in the high unemployment rates in the industries during periods of depression and the high prices which rule in them during periods of activity.

Moreover, not only is the demand for fixed capital from the point of view of the investor increased when trade is good, but the demand from the point of view of the producer of commodities is likewise increased. To bring about the construction of fixed capital an investor with savings available must agree with a producer who is prepared to use the fixed capital when constructed. The profit anticipated by the producer from the use of the fixed capital induces the investor to lay out his savings on the enterprise. When trade is good, profits are high, and at the same time producers wish to increase their output to meet the growing demand. Consequently, just at the time when there are more savings than usual there are more openings for investment than usual and higher profits to be expected from them. For example, it may be that in a particular industry the output increases, taken over a long period, at an average rate of 1 per cent per annum, and that the fixed capital requires renewal after twenty years' use. Then 5 per cent of the capital requires renewal each year and the demand for new plant will be 6 per cent of the total amount of plant when the increase of 1 per cent is allowed for. But if there is an expansion of trade which increases the output of this industry in a particular year by 4 per cent instead of 1 per cent, the new plant needed will be 9 per cent of the existing plant or no less than 50 per cent more than the average ; while if during a depression the output falls off by 2 per cent instead of increasing by 1 per cent, the new plant needed will be only 3 per cent of the existing plant or half the average. Of course the new plant produced would not coincide exactly with the amount needed on a proportional basis. The high prices ruling in the former case would induce manufacturers to make the best of their existing plant, while in the latter case the low prices would afford a good opportunity for effecting renewals, etc. But, however the full effect of this tendency may be mitigated, it is clear enough that all business connected with investment is in a class by itself so far as its responsiveness to trade fluctuations is concerned.

As the demand for new capital is the resultant of two distinct factors, the opening offered by the producer and the money offered by the investor, the business of dealing in investments is more complicated than other kinds of dealing. The dealers in investments are subdivided by a minute specialisation of function. For our present purpose, however, it is not necessary to enter into the distinction between stockbrokers and stockjobbers, underwriters and company promoters, finance companies and trust companies, or into the varieties of " somethings in the City " which prevail in the different commercial centres of the world. All the dealers in investments, all those people who intervene between the man with savings to invest on the one hand and the producer who needs fresh capital on the other, may be regarded collectively as the investment market. It is of the essence of the investment market that it does not invest, but *deals* in investments. Many of the individuals who are on the Stock Exchange or otherwise connected with the investment market will also be investors, but that is not their function in the market.

The investment market, and more especially that portion ordinarily called the Stock Exchange, makes a business of being able to sell and willing to buy any of the principal marketable securities. In order to do this they must so far as possible keep " working balances " of the principal securities which they undertake to sell, and they must so regulate the prices of the securities that the amount of each that they have in hand does not vary inconveniently. Of course this only applies to the Stock Exchange as a whole. No individual need aim at keeping a supply of every sort of security in his own hands ; he only need be able to communicate quickly with the man who has a supply of any given security. Now the capital value of the securities dealt in on any Stock Exchange is very large compared with the aggregate capital of the members. They are not, therefore, prepared to supply the necessary working balances of securities out of their own resources, and they borrow money from the banks to enable themselves to do so. And as the transactions in securities fluctuate widely from day to day and there is no definite period for which any given block of securities may be expected to be held, the money is usually lent from day to day or " at call." The stockjobber who borrows the money pays interest on the ascertained amount of his daily indebtedness. People who have saved money and wish to invest in marketable securities, rather than find openings privately, bring their savings to the Stock Exchange, and the investment of these savings diminishes the amount of securities in the hands of the Stock Exchange and correspondingly diminishes the aggregate indebtedness to the banks. The mere shuffling of investments, selling out to invest again, will not have any net effect in this direction. The working balances of securities are restored, however, and the indebtedness maintained by means of new issues of securities which pass through the Investment Market on their way to the investing public.

It is in regard to the new issues that the functions of the investment market have their chief importance, for it is the new issues which stand for an addition to the stock of fixed capital and which directly or indirectly use up the savings waiting for investment. A certain amount of risk always attends an attempt to find investors to take up shares in a new venture. It is impossible to be certain beforehand that the terms offered will be attractive enough to elicit a sufficient quantity of savings. To guard against the danger of the whole issue not being subscribed for, it is the practice to get some firm or company in the investment market to " underwrite " the shares, that is to undertake (in return for a commission of so much per cent on the whole issue) to take up such shares as are not subscribed for otherwise. If the whole issue is taken by the public the underwriters pocket the commission and the investment market is no more troubled with it except for the ordinary buying and selling transactions on the Stock Exchange. If the underwriters have to take a part of the issue themselves, however, this will not be with the intention of retaining it as a permanent investment, but they will look out for opportunities of disposing of it to investors when they can. A firm is only employed to underwrite an issue of shares if it has good credit, for if it has to take part of the issue it will have to borrow the money needed for the purpose. The mere fact that the shares have not been taken by the public will make them an unsatisfactory security to borrow on. An underwriting firm, therefore, may have a certain amount of difficulty in raising the money to enable it to discharge its obligations, unless it possesses ample resources.

Now at a time of expanding trade and growing inflation, when there is a general expectation of high profits and at the same time there is a flood of savings seeking investment, an underwriter's business yields a good profit at very little risk. But at the critical moment when the banks are compelled to intervene to reduce the inflation this is changed. There is a sudden diminution of profits which simultaneously checks the accumulation of savings and dispels the expectation of high profits. An underwriter may find that the diminution of savings upsets his calculations and leaves on his hands a quantity of securities for which before the tide turned he could have found a ready market, and that the prospect of disposing of these securities grows less and less with the steady shrinkage in the demand for investments and the failing prospect of high dividends. It must be remembered that, when trade is good, one of the contributory causes of the high profits is the sluggishness of wages in responding to the general upward movement of money values. The investor does not distinguish between the several factors which combine to produce high dividends in the industry in which he purposes to venture his savings, and it often happens, therefore, that the market price of shares includes the capitalised value of this ephemeral and indeed illegitimate form of profit. When wages have risen and prices have begun to fall this element of value melts away and the prices of securities depreciate. And recent issues will suffer most, for they will have been on the whole less favourable openings for investment than those of which advantage had been taken before, and the speculative and unsound ventures will not have been eliminated from among them. All business will experience a falling off of profits in consequence of the slackening demand, but, other things being equal, the businesses which have been in existence for some time and have· already survived previous trade depressions will get through with a smaller curtailment of output than new businesses which have hardly had time to establish a connexion. And as we have seen, the fixed capital which comprises the assets represented by the securities is subject to greater oscillations of money value than almost any other form of wealth.[1]

It will be seen, then, that of all the borrowers from the banks those who borrow for the purposes of the investment market are the most liable to failure when the period of good trade comes to an end. And as it happens, it is they who are most at the mercy of the banks in times of trouble. For it is their habit to borrow from day to day, and the banks, since they cannot call in loans to traders which will only mature after several weeks or months, are apt to try to reduce an excess of credit money by refusing to lend from day to day. If that happens the investment market will suddenly have to find the money which the banks want. The total amount of ready money in the hands of the whole investment market will probably be quite small, and, except in so far as they can persuade the banks to wait (in consideration probably of a high rate of interest), they must raise money by selling securities. But there are limits to the amount that can be raised in this way. The demand for investments is very inelastic. The money offered at any time is ordinarily simply the amount of the accumulated savings of the community till then uninvested. This total can only be added to by people investing sums which they would otherwise leave as part of their working balances of money,

[1] It must be remembered that though the capital value of an investment yielding a fixed rate of interest *falls* slightly when prices are rising, the capital value of an investment yielding a variable dividend *rises*, since rising prices mean high dividends.

and they cannot be induced to increase their investments very much in this way, however low the price in proportion to the yield of the securities offered. Consequently when the banks curtail the accommodation which they give to the investment market and the investment market tries to raise money by selling securities, the prices of securities may fall heavily without attracting much additional money. Meanwhile the general fall in the prices of securities will undermine the position of the entire investment market, since the value of the assets held against their liabilities to the banks will be depreciated. If the banks insist on payment in such circumstances a multitude of failures on the Stock Exchange and in the investment market must follow. The knowledge of this will deter the banks from making the last turn of the screw if they can help it. But it may be that the banks themselves are acting under dire necessity. If they have let the creation of credit money get beyond their control, if they are on the point of running short of the legal tender money necessary to meet the daily demands upon them, they may have no alternative but to insist on payment. When the collapse comes it is not unlikely that some of the banks themselves will be dragged down by it. A bank which has suffered heavy losses may be unable any longer to show an excess of assets over liabilities, and if subjected to heavy demands may be unable to borrow to meet them.

The calling in of loans from the investment market enables the banks to reduce the excess credit money rapidly. The failure of one or more banks, by annihilating the credit money based upon their demand liabilities, hastens the process still more. A crisis

therefore has the effect of bringing a trade depression
into being with striking suddenness. In the chain of
events the actual crisis would probably occur some
little time after the reaction from the preceding period
of active trade has begun. But this is not necessarily
the case. For the increase of wages tends to encroach
on profits even while trade is still expanding and prices
rising. There may then be a shrinkage in savings at
that stage, the investment market may get choked up
with securities for which there is an insufficient demand,
and the collapse may occur while the activity of trade
is still unimpaired.

It should not escape attention that even in a financial
crisis, which is ordinarily regarded as simply a " collapse
of credit," credit only plays a secondary part. The
shortage of savings, which curtails the demand for
investments, and the excess of credit money, which
leads the banks to call in their loans, are causes at least
as prominent as the impairment of credit. And the
impairment of credit itself is not a mere capricious loss
of confidence, but is a revised estimate of the profits of
commercial enterprises in general, which is based on the
palpable facts of the market. The wholesale depreciation of securities at such a time is not due to a vague
" distrust," but partly to the plain fact that the money
values of the assets which they represent are falling and
partly to forced sales necessitated by the sudden
demand for money. Nor is the demand for money
itself a sign of failing confidence. The banks want to
reduce their demand liabilities, because those liabilities
necessitate a larger supply of legal tender money than
they can collect, and the legal tender money is needed
for the ordinary practical needs of commerce. Of course

distrust of a business means an expectation that it will fail, and as there are many failures during a crisis there must be distrust in so far as those failures are foreseen. It is true also that distrust of a business begets an unwillingness to lend and the inability to borrow itself hastens the failure of the business distrusted. But nevertheless the crisis does not *originate* in distrust. Loss of credit in fact is only a symptom.

. . . . . .

It will be observed that our theory as to the origination of trade fluctuations depends ultimately on the correspondence of the calculated effects of the assumed causes with the known characteristics of the fluctuations. We have now shown that the monetary organisation of the world might be expected to engender just such periodic fluctuations as do actually occur. To complete the argument we ought to follow this conclusion up with a statistical investigation tracing the correspondence of the recorded facts with the theory. This would be a gigantic undertaking and would need a far bulkier and more ambitious volume than the present work. And the phenomena of trade fluctuations are so well established that economists and statisticians on the one hand and business men on the other are all likely to agree as to whether the correspondence is established. At the same time I do not underestimate the value and importance of such an investigation, even with the rather insufficient statistical material which alone is available. In the absence of statistical verification I can only submit the views set forth in the preceding pages for what they are worth.

XVII

BANKING AND CURRENCY LEGISLATION IN RELATION TO THE STATE OF TRADE

THE preceding chapters have been devoted to an investigation of the manner in which trade fluctuations are generated under the banking and currency systems which actually prevail in the world at the present time. Having established the inherent tendency towards fluctuations under those systems we might leave the subject at this point. But there is another very important class of influences to be taken into account, that is to say, the legislative and administrative action of the Sovereign State. That action falls into three distinct categories. First, the State is responsible for the banking and currency system of the country. Even where it leaves these matters entirely unregulated, as has, for instance, been practically the case in China, it is still responsible for *not* taking action. In drawing attention here to the effect of State action upon fluctuations I do not mean to refer to the responsibility of the State for maintaining banking and currency institutions under which fluctuations may arise. That is a subject already dealt with. The State action now in point is that which is directed to an *alteration* in the law or practice of banking and currency. Such action may have far-reaching effects on the state of trade not only in the country directly concerned, but throughout the world.

The second form of State action which we shall have to consider is that which is concerned with the taxing power, and more especially with the imposition or increase and the removal or decrease of a protective tariff. The third is concerned with the functions of the State as the manager of large sums of money, that is to say, with Government Finance. These two latter subjects will be dealt with in Chapters XVIII and XIX. The present chapter will be occupied with the State regulation of banking and currency. This subject is intimately connected with that of the supply of the precious metals, which was discussed in Chapter X. It was then pointed out that the annual supply of gold is not great enough relatively to the accumulated stock of gold to occasion short-period fluctuations of trade, but that changes in the annual supply may have important effects over long periods. The history of currency throughout the world during the past half-century has been greatly affected by the history of gold-mining and silver-mining in the same period. The production of silver has increased steadily, but the production of gold has been subject to great variations. The gold discoveries in America and Australia just before 1850 enormously increased the annual output, and for twenty-five years after that date the annual supply of gold was far beyond anything of which the world had till then had experience. About 1875, however, the mines began to show signs of diminished yield, and for twenty years after that date the annual supply was about 5,000,000 oz. as compared with the 6,000,000 or 7,000,000 till then yielded. In the 'nineties there was again a rapid increase, attributable partly to the discovery and development of the Transvaal mines and partly to the invention of new processes. The annual supply has increased ever since (subject to a temporary set-back in 1900 owing to the closing of the South African mines during the war) and has now reached the enormous total of 22,000,000 oz. or nearly £100,000,000 worth.

Fifty years ago the world's currency, taken as a whole, was bimetallic. There were (as there still are) countries which used inconvertible paper and there were many monometallic states. England already had a gold standard. Many countries, especially in the East, had silver standards. But in the majority of European nations the free or practically free coinage of both gold and silver in unlimited quantities prevailed. Where a metal is coined on application practically without charge and without limitation of quantity it must circulate at its bullion value. If it is worth more as bullion than as coin, coin will be melted into bullion, and if it is worth more as coin than as bullion, bullion will be presented for coinage. In fact under such a system a coin is nothing more than an ingot of metal of which the weight and fineness are certified by the Government. Where both gold and silver are coined on application *both* will circulate at their bullion value. The inconvenience of having two independent units of money[1] would be serious, and it was therefore the practice in countries with a bimetallic system of currency to prescribe a ratio between the gold and silver units. The amount of gold in a French 20-franc piece and the amount of silver in a 5-franc piece were both prescribed by law, and it was also prescribed by law that the one should be legal tender for twenty francs and the

[1] This was largely the practice till the nineteenth century.

other for 5 francs. The gold franc unit was legal tender for the same amount as the silver franc unit, and as the weight of silver in the latter was 15½ times the weight of gold in the former, the effect of the law was to secure that gold should be worth 15½ times as much as silver in France. So long as gold and silver were circulating side by side under these conditions the ratio of the market value of the two metals could never diverge far from the legal coinage ratio. For this could only occur if the market value of one or other or both metals diverged from its value as coin, and that divergence, as we have seen, would be rapidly corrected by the presentation for coinage of the metal which is overvalued as coin or the melting down of the metal which is undervalued as coin. Thus, if there were a sudden increase in the supply of gold the consequence, apart from the legal regulation of the ratio, would be a fall in the value of gold and consequently in the ratio. But if gold coin is worth more than gold bullion when reckoned in silver, gold will be continually presented for coinage ; the quantity of currency will be increased ; the prices of commodities and in particular of gold and silver bullion will rise ; as the gold is coined the quantity of gold bullion in the market will be decreased and the price of gold bullion will rise more than in proportion to the prices of other commodities ; as the price of silver bullion rises, silver will become worth less as coin than as bullion and silver coin will be melted, thus increasing the supply of silver bullion, the price of which will rise *less* than in proportion to the prices of other commodities. These processes will go on until the ratio between the market prices of the metals is again equal to the legal ratio. The net result will have been that the new gold has to a great extent *displaced* the silver coinage. So long as there is any nation in the world with an effective bimetallic system, that is to say, a system under which both metals are actually coined and circulated together, the market prices of the metals will be all over the world approximately in the ratio there legally established.[1] But it may happen that there is so great an increase in the supply of one of the two metals as to displace the other metal altogether from the coinages of all the bimetallic countries in the world. If this occurs the legal ratio ceases to be operative, and the bimetallic countries become practically monometallic users of the metal so cheapened.

Precisely the same effect may be produced by an increased demand for one of the two metals. This actually occurred when the newly constituted German Empire decided in 1871 to adopt a gold standard. The increased supplies of gold in the preceding twenty years had been accompanied by increased supplies of silver and the bimetallic system in Europe had remained unimpaired. As it turned out, however, the system failed to stand the strain of the substitution of gold for silver as the metal in ordinary use in Germany. Till then the German States had been mainly silver-using, and only about 7 per cent of their aggregate standard coinage was gold. The adoption of the gold standard meant the ultimate issue of additional gold coin to the value of something like £100,000,000. Of course, this

---

[1] Incidentally it follows that there cannot exist simultaneously effective bimetallic systems in two countries with appreciably different ratios. As a matter of fact, the legal ratio in the United States, 16 to 1, undervalued silver in terms of gold as compared with the European bimetallic systems, and consequently the silver standard dollar did not in practice circulate there.

could only be done over a series of years. The old silver thaler only ceased to be unlimited legal tender in 1876, by which time gold to the value of nearly £70,000,000 had been issued. But the rate of progress was quite sufficient to cause something like a gold famine. As it happened, two of the great bimetallic countries which would ordinarily have possessed large stocks of metal currency were under an inconvertible paper regime at the time. The United States, which owing to the legal undervaluation of silver was practically on a monometallic gold basis, had suspended the payment of its notes in specie in 1862, shortly after the outbreak of the Civil War, and the notes had been at a discount ever since. France, likewise under the stress of war, had suspended the payment of Bank of France notes in 1870 and had exported much of the large gold reserve usually held by the bank. Italy, Austria, Russia, and Spain were also using inconvertible paper, so that the region within which bimetallism was effective was really very small. The displacement of gold by silver began to be felt towards the end of 1872, when Denmark, Norway, and Sweden adopted the gold standard, while Holland found it necessary to suspend the free coinage of silver. The " Latin Union," composed of France, Italy, Belgium, Greece and Switzerland, followed suit by limiting the coinage of the standard silver pieces of five francs to a certain fixed aggregate in 1874, a measure renewed from year to year till the issue of these coins was finally stopped by an agreement arrived at in 1878. Meanwhile, France and the United States were preparing for a resumption of specie payments, and this was accomplished by both practically on a gold basis in 1878. In France, as we have already seen, the 5-franc piece, though no longer coined, remained unlimited legal tender. In the United States not only was the silver dollar made unlimited legal tender, but provision was made for the coinage of a limited quantity of new silver dollars every month. In the seven years, however, from 1871 to 1878, the entire system of bimetallism had really been swept away. The old ratio of 15½ to 1, which had prevailed in the bimetallic states and had therefore governed the relative values of gold and silver all over the world, had vanished, and the market ratio had reached 18 to 1. The East continued to use silver, but in the West the demand for metal for coinage was concentrated exclusively on gold, of which the supply had just begun to fall off. Even the nations which still had inconvertible paper currencies began to aim at accumulating gold reserves with a view to the resumption of specie payments. The coincidence of these measures with the shortage of the gold supply between 1875 and 1890 led to a very heavy fall in the prices of commodities. Mr. Sauerbeck's " Index Number," which expresses the general level of prices in England from time to time as a percentage of the average level for the ten years, 1867 to 1877, fell steadily and reached a minimum of 59 in July, 1896.

The continued coinage of silver dollars in the United States, even though limited, was almost the only important currency measure which tended to mitigate the general gold famine. In practice the dollars themselves were usually not issued, but " silver certificates " were used for circulation instead, and under the amending legislation of 1890 the formality of coining was dispensed with, the silver being bought to the amount of 4,500,000 oz. a month and paid for in " Treasury notes," which were legal tender, just like the existing United States notes or " greenbacks." During the 'eighties the effect of the issue of silver certificates was partly counteracted by a contraction of the bank-note circulation, but after 1890 this ceased to be the case and the full effect of the increase of the legal tender paper in displacing gold began to be felt. Large sums of gold were exported, and in 1893, when the gold basis of the currency was found to be endangered by the depletion of the stock of gold, there was an acute financial crisis and the issue of notes against silver was brought hurriedly to an end. Thenceforward the entire needs of the Western World for fresh standard currency had to be met from the annual output of gold. And just then, as it happened, the output of gold began to increase. In 1892 it reached 7,000,000 oz., an amount in excess of that annually produced in the period before 1875. By 1899 it amounted to no less than 14,800,000 oz., and in 1903, after the end of the war in South Africa, to 15,800,000 oz., while in 1912 the output exceeded 22,000,000 oz. The gold standard systems adopted in the 'seventies have been maintained, and the increase in the gold supply has facilitated the passage to a gold standard of countries like Russia, Austria, and Italy, which during the gold famine had vainly endeavoured to absorb inflated issues of legal tender paper. The rise in the prices of commodities since 1896 has been almost as marked as the fall in the years preceding that date. Whereas Mr. Sauerbeck's index number fell to 59·2 in 1896, the lowest point touched during the depression which followed the American crisis of 1907 was 71·9.

We must now examine the bearing of these relatively long-period changes upon the theory of fluctuations. For this purpose it is necessary to consider them in connexion with the other long-period changes which formed the subject of Chapter X. If wealth and population were stationary there would be no need for additions to the world's currency.

Every day a certain number of people pass out of the ranks of the working population on account of age, infirmity, or other reasons. Every day a certain number of young people reach the age at which they begin work. In virtue of the tendency of population to increase the gains exceed the losses. If work is to be found for the additional working population there will be a proportional increase in the output of commodities, and consequently also in the demand for borrowed money to finance industry and in the demand for legal tender money to pay wages. These latter demands the banks will not be prepared to meet unless there is a proportional increase in the stock of legal tender money. If we assume for the moment the absence of monetary disturbances and of the consequent fluctuations, then so long as existing prices and money values remain unaltered the trade of the country can absorb only so much of the new supply of labour as the increase in the stock of legal tender money will provide for. If the increase is insufficient to provide for all, those unprovided for will go to swell the total of the unemployed or will displace people till then in employment. In fact, though the new recruits all contribute in a sense to the aggregate demand for commodities, only those who earn money contribute to the aggregate *effective* demand. The demand emanating from those who have no money counts for nothing in the organisation of industry. But of course the increase in the unemployed sets up a tendency towards lower wages, and as this tendency makes itself felt, prices fall, the demand for commodities increases, and the surplus labour is absorbed.

On the other hand, if the supply of currency is increasing more rapidly than the supply of labour there will be a tendency for the prices of commodities to rise continually, and, still apart from any question of monetary disturbances, there will be a chronic state of good trade.

In practice these tendencies are important not so much in themselves as when superimposed on a trade fluctuation. When trade is on the down grade, and there is at the same time an insufficient supply of new currency, the number of unemployed will be increased by the natural increase of the working population. The severity of the distress, which furnishes the inducement to accept lower wages, will be correspondingly intensified, and the fall of wages will no doubt be accelerated. The depression will be either more prolonged, or more severe, or both more prolonged and more severe, than it would have been but for the scarcity of currency. And in the same circumstances the period of revival will be less prolonged, or less pronounced, or both. An abundant supply of new currency will have the contrary effect, mitigating a depression and stimulating and prolonging a revival of trade.

In practice the long-period price changes, while they have not been large enough to disturb the course of the ordinary trade fluctuations very seriously, have been by no means negligible. Again employing Mr. Sauerbeck's index numbers, we find the following comparisons between the price levels in years of minimum trade. Each of the years selected is one in the trough of a depression when prices were at their lowest, and they are therefore fairly comparable :—

Year	Index Number
1849	74
1858	91
1870	96
1879	83
1887	68
1896	61
1903	69
1908	73

In the nine years from 1849 to 1858, immediately after the gold discoveries in Australia and California, prices rose by 2 per cent per annum. In the next twelve years, 1858–70, they rose by less than ½ per cent per annum. In 1871 the abandonment of bimetallism began with the German Gold Standard Law, and in 1873 the gold supply fell below 5,000,000 oz. In the nine years 1870–9 prices fell by about 1½ per cent per annum, and in the eight years 1879–87 by 2¼ per cent per annum. In 1892 the gold supply began to revive, and in the nine years 1887–96 the fall was little more than 1 per cent per annum, and in the seven years 1896–1903 the fall was replaced by a rise of nearly 2 per cent, and prices have continued to rise, though at a diminishing rate, since then. Thus the long-period variations of prices have usually progressed at a rate of between 1 and 2 per cent per annum.

And as a matter of fact, during the gold famine from 1873 to 1896 the periods of depression were long and severe while the periods of good trade were short and incomplete. The financial crisis of 1873 ushered in a period of bad trade which persisted until 1881. The revival which began in that year was of no great extent and only lasted till 1883, when there ensued another severe set-back. A more pronounced recovery took place in 1889, but this in turn came to an end in 1892 and trade remained very bad till 1896. The period of good trade which began in 1896 lasted till 1901 and was longer and more substantial than any since 1873. It is true that the depression which followed lasted till the end of 1905 and was therefore as long as those of 1892–6, and 1884–8, but it was conspicuously less severe than either of these latter. The revival that followed lasted only two years, since it collapsed at the end of 1907, but then the corresponding depression was equally short, being practically over by the end of 1909, when the present period of good trade may be said to have begun.

Experience suggests that a scarcity of new gold prolongs the periods of depression and an abundance of new gold shortens them, so that the whole period of a fluctuation is somewhat shorter in the latter circumstances than in the former. The rapid oscillations between 1849 and 1873 seem to confirm this, though the statistical information for that period is rather insufficient, and trade was harassed throughout the period by repeated wars.

Another consequence of long-period changes in the gold supply deserves mention, though its connexion with trade fluctuations is less direct. This is the effect on the rate of interest. We have seen that short-period price changes, so far as they are foreseen, affect the rate of interest for short loans. The expectation of long-period price changes must affect the rate of interest on permanent investments. If prices are going to fall for the next twenty years at the rate of 1 per cent per annum, and if the natural rate of interest is $3\frac{1}{2}$ per cent, the right to receive £3 10s. per annum will be worth much more than £100. For if £100 were expended on fixed capital the yield would initially be £3 10s., but the commodities produced would drop in value every year till after twenty years they would be worth only about 80 per cent of £3 10s. or £2 16s. The right to receive £3 10s. in money in perpetuity is worth more than the right to receive annual consignments of commodities which are now worth £3 10s. but which in the future will be worth something less. At the same time it must be admitted not only that it is difficult to form a reliable opinion as to what the output of gold and the world's currency systems will be twenty years hence, but that as a matter of fact the people who deal in investments know and care nothing about the purchasing power of money. Does it follow then that the relation of the production of gold to the rate of interest is a matter of academic theory ? By no means ; for the people who deal in investments do pay the closest attention to the profits of business, as shown by experience, and those profits *are* affected by price movements. In fact it is the *past* output of gold, not the future output, which really affects the rate of interest. This is clearly seen when the actual movements in the prices of securities are examined. The price of Consols started to rise after the collapse of trade which occurred in 1873, and rose steadily (except for slight reactions during the trade revivals of 1881–3 and 1889–91) till it reached a maximum in 1897, i.e. in a year when the output of gold had for some time been increasing and had reached the total, till then unparalleled, of 11,420,000 oz. The high price was unaffected by any expectation of a high " profit rate " simply because no one ever thought of considering what effect on the yield of capital the increased gold production would have. But the price *was* affected by the experience of investments during the long gold famine when profits had been low almost for a generation, and indeed it may be regarded as the outcome of this experience. In the same way the low prices of securities at the present time are the product of the contrary experience, the great output of gold in the last twenty years having been accompanied by inflated profits.[1]

But besides these long-period changes there are other currency measures which are of a character to have a more direct and immediate effect on the state of trade. For example, it often happens that a nation which ordinarily uses a metallic currency resorts, under stress of war or for some similar reason, to the issue of in-convertible paper. If this is done by a large and important nation the quantity of gold displaced may be sufficient of itself to occasion an abnormal activity of trade in the surrounding countries. The United States issued inconvertible paper in excessive quantities during the Civil War, and France suspended specie payments during the war of 1870. In both cases the effect seems to have been rather to intensify an

---

[1] It is of some interest to note that the average rate of discount for three months bills during the ten years 1888-97 was 2·17 per cent, while the yield of Consols at the average market price for 1897 was 2·25 per cent. For the ten years ended 1911 the average rate of discount was 3·07 per cent, and the yield of Consols in 1911 was 3·15 per cent.

expansion of trade already under way, than to cause an independent fluctuation. It is likewise true that the simultaneous resumption of cash payments by both nations in 1878 increased the severity of the trade depression which then prevailed.

It often happens that when a period of inflation has resulted in a crisis, Governments are induced to take emergency measures for relieving the scarcity of legal tender currency which is characteristic of such conditions. Provided this is done only when the state of crisis is really in being, and provided the rate of interest on temporary loans is kept up high enough to secure a steady contraction of credit money, it is a perfectly justifiable measure. It will enable the banks to carry out the contraction gradually, whereas this can be effected suddenly only at the cost of widespread bankruptcies. But if the issue of emergency currency (presumably in the form of legal tender paper) is made prematurely in order to stave off the crisis and the rate of interest is not raised, it is likely only to make the crisis more severe when it comes, and the subsequent return to a metallic currency will be all the more painful.

It is not necessary to attempt an exhaustive examination of all the banking and currency measures by means of which a Government may intentionally or unintentionally influence the state of trade. The only other case that calls for special mention is that of legislation facilitating or impeding the use of credit money. The use of credit money cannot, as a rule, be increased in a country merely by legislation. It depends more upon the habits of the people than upon laws or regulations. But it may happen that some vexatious legal obstacle to the free use of credit money is removed in response to a strong popular demand. In such a case the creation of a flood of credit money would cause an abnormal expansion of trade, and the export of superfluous gold would spread the effects far and wide.

XVIII

The Government in its capacity of the taxing authority does not for the most part seriously affect the course of trade fluctuations. But to this rule there is to be found one very important exception in protective tariffs. Protective tariffs are avowedly imposed for the purpose of affecting trade as well as producing revenue, and it will be found that they are of material importance in trade fluctuations.

It was shown in Chapter IX that the *existence* of a tariff really has very little effect on a trade movement. The two or three consequences then deduced were none of them very momentous. But we are concerned in the present chapter with a *change* in a tariff. The imposition or increase and the removal or decrease of a protective tariff involve very complicated adjustments which we must now proceed to investigate.

First, we will consider the case of the imposition of a new tariff, or the increase of an existing tariff, in any country with a gold standard. For the sake of simplicity we will assume that the tariff is applied impartially to all imported goods at approximately the same rates. The immediate effect of the new tariff will be that foreign producers can no longer accept orders at the same prices as before except at a sacrifice of profit and probably at an actual loss. The dealers in goods all or part of the supply of which is imported (which for brevity may be called " import commodities ") will find that they cannot replenish their stocks on as favourable terms as before. The domestic producer will be able to take the same orders as before at the old prices, but the foreign producer will ask prices higher by all or part of the new import duties. In preference to paying these increased prices the dealers will give larger orders to the domestic producers. The domestic producers will be prepared to increase their output. If their plant is already fully employed they will probably only do so in return for some increase of price. If their plant is not fully employed they may be ready to take some increase of orders without any increase of price. It is unlikely, except in particular trades where the proportion of goods obtained from abroad is small, that the entire demand can be supplied with no increase of price. At the same time the foreign producer will find his business curtailed. He will receive the same orders from his own country as before, but his profit on the goods which have to pay the increased tariff will probably be turned into a loss. Rather than face the large diminution of output involved in the entire abandonment of this branch of his trade, he will offer goods at a price increased by something less than the amount of the import duty. A new equilibrium will be reached in the trade in import commodities ; the domestic supply will be increased ; the foreign supply will be diminished ; the wholesale prices will be increased ; the prices received by the foreign producers (being the wholesale prices *less* the import duties) will be diminished. But, of course, the dealers cannot as a permanent arrangement pay the increased wholesale price out of their own pockets. There must, sooner or later, be a corresponding rise in retail prices. This is none the less so if there is a ring or combination among the dealers with complete control of prices, for the scale of prices likely to secure the highest profit to the ring will be higher than before. This increase in retail prices will involve some diminution in the demand for import commodities. The domestic producer will still be able to find a market for a larger output and yet at a higher wholesale price than before, and the foreign producer will still have a smaller share even of the diminished demand and will get less money for the goods he does sell.

But obviously this equilibrium, based on a greatly diminished importation of foreign goods, can only be temporary. Nothing has happened as yet to affect the volume of the export trade, and therefore the balance of exports and imports will have been upset. The excess of exports will give rise to a growing indebtedness from abroad. This growing indebtedness cannot be left outstanding. Indeed, the demand for loans in the protected country is actually stimulated, since the protected trades need more borrowed money to finance their increased output, and probably more fixed capital to enable them to increase their output beyond the capacities of their existing plant. The foreign investor will wish to transmit money to take advantage of these opportunities, and thus to the indebtedness from abroad arising from the excess of exports of goods will be added a further indebtedness arising from the exports of securities.

The rate of exchange will have to be adjusted, and (unless the increase of tariff is merely trifling) it will go to the import specie point and gold will begin to be imported. The import of gold must go on until the balance between exports and imports is restored. The tendency to restore the balance is obvious enough. As the gold arrives the banks proceed to build up credit money upon it. The purchasing power of the community is correspondingly increased, all the phenomena of good trade ensue and prices rise, not only the prices of the import commodities, but the prices of everything else as well. As the prices of the import commodities rise, the effect of the increased tariff in excluding foreign goods is diminished. At the same time the rise in the prices of other commodities diverts a portion of the goods previously exported, to meet the domestic demand.

The position of the commodities part of the supply of which is exported (which may be called the " export commodities ") deserves careful consideration. The rise in the price of the protected import commodities does not necessarily diminish the effective demand for other commodities. In the case of a commodity the demand for which is technically " elastic " an increase in price means an actual decrease in the aggregate amount of money spent upon it. But taking any miscellaneous selection of commodities, if there is a general increase in their prices (with no accompanying increase in the money to be spent on all commodities together) the presumption is that the inelastic demand will prevail over the elastic and the aggregate of money spent on the commodities of which the prices have increased will be greater, leaving less to be spent on the remaining commodities. It is probable, therefore, that apart from the increase in purchasing power due to the importation of gold the increase of price in the import commodities would lead to more money being spent by the consumer on those commodities and less on other commodities. But if that is so, then initially exports will actually be stimulated and all the more gold will have to be imported to restore the balance of exports and imports. From the mere fact that the reduction of exports is effected by an increased domestic demand and not by a failure of the foreign demand, it follows that at this stage the producers of export commodities will be experiencing good trade, though, of course, not so good as the protected producers of import commodities.

When the diminution of exports and the increase of imports have gone far enough the importation of gold will cease. But even then permanent equilibrium will not have been reached. For the general increase of prices will have upset the balance between wages and profits. If money wages have not increased, real wages will have diminished through the fall in the purchasing power of money. Finding that that is the case and that their employers' profits are very high, the workmen will begin to press for an increase of money wages. Some increase the employers will be in a position to grant. But as soon as wages rise the demands on the banks for legal tender money will begin to grow. The reaction from good trade to bad will set in. There will no doubt follow the endless cycle of fluctuations which we have already proved to be the natural sequel. With the details of those fluctuations we are not here concerned. But it should be observed that the future normal or average position about which trade oscillates will be modified. The import commodities will be at higher prices at home than abroad, while the export commodities will be at the same prices at home as abroad. There will be permanently a greater stock of gold in the country than before the increase of tariff, and money wages will be correspondingly higher. The imports of foreign goods and exports of domestic goods will both be permanently diminished. The domestic production of the import commodities will be permanently increased and the domestic production of the export commodities will be permanently diminished. In the first reaction from the period of good trade caused by the increase of the tariff these changes will make themselves felt.

The prices of import commodities will fall as much as those of export commodities, but they will start at a relatively higher level and will stop at a relatively higher level. The domestic producers of import commodities will start with exceptionally high profits which will give them a margin to cover both the rise of wages and the fall of prices. The producers of export commodities will find that their goods fall to the same prices as in former periods of depression and will in addition have to pay the increased rate of money wages. Thus the burden of the trade depression will be thrown on the export businesses. There will be little unemployment among the workmen engaged in producing the import commodities, but there will be a double allowance of unemployment among those engaged in producing the export commodities. The fall of wages which occurs in these conditions will therefore be more rapid among the latter than among the former. There will be a tendency for workmen to pass from the one set of trades into the other, but this can only take place gradually and it may be many years before industry has completely accommodated itself to the new conditions.

From the preceding exposition it follows that the imposition of a new protective tariff or the increase of an existing protective tariff does occasion an expansion of trade. As to whether it is a desirable measure, that is a highly controversial question. But to avoid misunderstanding it will be well to point out that it is only a *change* in the direction of higher protection that has this effect and the effect soon exhausts itself; the mere *existence* of a tariff, high or low, unchanged has no such effect. Repeated resort to this expedient for stimulating trade means ever higher and higher protection, and when the protection is so high as to be practically prohibitive a further increase no longer produces any result. Moreover, it must not be supposed that " good " trade is an unmixed blessing. It is true that it is very profitable to capital, but the high profits are obtained at the expense of labour. The waste due to unemployment is avoided, but employment is good merely because real wages are low, and much of what the working classes gain from full employment they lose through the high cost of living. And as soon as wages accommodate themselves to the rise of prices the stimulus to trade ceases altogether.

The consequences of the removal or reduction of a protective tariff may be dealt with in the same way. The first result will be that dealers in import commodities will be able to get their foreign supplies cheaper than before ; they will tend to give orders to the foreign producer and the domestic producer will have to accept lower prices. The prices actually received by the foreign producers will be increased, since the duty has no longer to be subtracted from the ruling wholesale price. The increase of imports involves a growing balance of indebtedness to foreign countries, which can only be corrected by an adjustment of the rate of exchange. The rate of exchange will move to the export specie point and gold will be exported. The diminishing purchasing power will lead to a diminishing domestic demand for the export commodities, and a greater proportion of the output of those commodities will be exported. At the same time the diminishing demand for the import commodities will lead to a smaller importation. The general contraction of demand will present all the features of a trade depression, and so long as money wages remain undiminished there will be unemployment, especially among the producers of import commodities. But, of course, the general fall of prices means an increased purchasing power of wages. Workmen can accept a reduction of money wages without being placed in a less favourable position than before the change, and the prevalence of unemployment gives them, as is always the case during a trade depression, an inducement to do so. But, as in the contrary case of an increase in the tariff, it will be some time and there may be several oscillations in trade before the industrial conditions have accommodated themselves to the change. Till then the workmen engaged in the production of the import commodities will be in a less favourable position than those engaged in the production of the export commodities.

Thus, just as an increase in a protective tariff gives rise to an expansion of trade, so a decrease in a protective tariff causes a depression. Both alike are quite transitory in character. But even so these two facts completely explain the tendency of nearly all countries, sooner or later, to adopt protection and the extreme difficulty they experience in getting rid of a protective tariff when it has once been set up. Either increase or decrease of the tariff causes some unsettlement of existing interests, but whereas an increase occasions an immediate gain to traders a decrease occasions an immediate loss.

When any country adopts a change of tariff the effect on its neighbours is the contrary of the effect on itself, though ordinarily so much diluted that it is of much less importance. When there is a very widespread movement towards increased protection the country or countries which do not follow the fashion may suffer quite a serious trade depression from the absorption of gold by the protected countries. England was to some extent in this position during and just after the gold scarcity from 1873 to 1890, and that no doubt is the explanation of the very low rate of interest and high prices of securities which prevailed in England as compared with other countries during that period.

Measures of taxation other than protective tariffs are not for the most part of much importance to our subject. There is, however, one other such measure which deserves mention. At the present time it is the practice in the majority of countries to raise the money necessary for local as distinguished from national administration by a tax on real property. Real property for this purpose comprises, on the one hand, structures and improvements, including dwelling-houses, factories, and most forms of fixed capital, and on the other hand all economic rent or "land values." A movement exists for relieving real property of the former class wholly or partly from the liability for local taxation and transferring the burden on to the land values. Assume that this step is taken in a country where the existing burden on property is 25 per cent of the annual value, and let the prevailing rate of interest be 4 per cent, so that property is worth 25 years' purchase of its net annual value. If the entire burden is transferred to land values or provided for in any other way which will relieve the structures and improvements, the yield of fixed capital and the rents of dwelling-houses will suddenly be raised from 4 to 5 per cent of the capital cost, the extra 1 per cent being the portion hitherto paid by way of taxation. All openings for investment in fixed capital will become more profitable than before in this proportion, and the country concerned will attract a much larger proportion of the world's savings now that it can pay 5 per cent instead of 4.[1]

Foreign investors will wish to take advantage of the opportunity offered for employing their savings profitably. In order to do so the money must be transmitted in the ordinary way by bills of exchange, until the demand for bills abroad drives the rate of exchange to the import specie point. Gold will then be imported until the increase in purchasing power at home has stimulated imports and diminished exports so far that the divergence between them covers the sums remitted

[1] It may be pointed out that this tendency will be in no way interfered with by the increased burdens on economic rent. Economic rent is merely the fee paid for occupying space; the space cannot be manufactured, and has no "cost of production"; a burden placed upon it cannot diminish the supply of space nor can the removal of such a burden stimulate the supply.

from abroad for investment. Meanwhile the trades connected with the construction of houses and fixed capital will receive more than the usual number of orders and contracts. Employment in these trades will be very good, the prices offered will be high, and profits and wages will grow correspondingly, and this state of things will continue until all the most profitable openings for investment in houses and fixed capital have been used up. At first the importation of gold and the rise of prices will stimulate all trades alike, but as soon as a sufficient supply of gold has been obtained this effect will cease, and only the trades directly concerned in the provision of houses and fixed capital will benefit. Finally, when the attractions to investors have been used up these latter trades also will revert to their normal condition. The extra gold which came in at the beginning of the process will be sent away at the end, and the return to normal conditions will accordingly be accompanied by the phenomena of depression. This being so, any reform of taxation which aims at relieving the burdens imposed by local taxation on capital should be carried into effect gradually. If it is done too suddenly the violent expansion and subsequent contraction of trade will cause loss and distress.

XIX

PUBLIC FINANCE IN RELATION TO THE STATE OF TRADE

WE have now dealt with two of the three functions of Government which possess importance in the theory of fluctuations. There remains still to be considered the position of the Government as the recipient of a very large income. Incidental to this are all the complicated operations of Government finance, such as National Expenditure, the management of the Government banking accounts, Government borrowing, permanent and temporary, and the repayment or redemption of loans. These operations derive their importance not so much from being in the hands of the Executive, as from being carried on on an exceptionally large scale. They are not very different from the corresponding operations of an ordinary business firm or company, but in almost all countries the national revenue is far greater than the income of the largest business.

The question of precisely how much of the national wealth is taken by the Government in the form of taxation and spent on administration need not trouble us. If the Government wastes money that is a bad thing, but though it may make the country poorer it does not affect the state of trade.

On the other hand, the management of the Government banking accounts, which is a matter of far less intrinsic importance, happens to be of considerable interest in the theory of fluctuations. It is usual for the Government banking account in any country to be kept at the Central Bank, where such an institution exists. In England, for instance, public balances are kept (mainly) at the Bank of England ; in France, at the Bank of France ; in Germany, at the Reichsbank. Under this system the Government banking account figures among the demand liabilities of the Central Bank alongside the balances of other banks. Now it is usual for the Central Bank to keep its liabilities in a certain proportion to its holdings of cash. Consequently when the Government balance increases, the bank will take steps to effect a reduction in its other demand liabilities and along with the rest in the balances of the other banks. The other banks regard their balances with the Central Bank as their reserves and so they in turn will try to reduce their demand liabilities. Thus a casual increase in Government balances sometimes has quite a perceptible effect on the state of trade. And a casual decrease likewise may have the contrary effect of stimulating trade. This arises entirely from the practice of keeping the Government's banking account with the Central Bank. Suppose, for example, that the Government balance is £5,000,000 and the balances of the other banks with the Central Bank come to a total of £30,000,000 ; and suppose that the banks have cash holdings on their own premises to the amount of £50,000,000, making reserves of £80,000,000 in all, and that their aggregate demand liabilities are £800,000,000. If the Government receives payments in excess of disbursements to the amount of £5,000,000 the demand liabilities of the banks will be reduced to £795,000,000 and the Government balance will be increased to £10,000,000. The Central Bank, however, is not prepared to let its demand liabilities increase by £5,000,000 and it puts up the rate of interest. Probably it will not think it necessary to bring back its demand liabilities precisely to the old figure, but will be satisfied when they have been reduced by, say, £4,000,000. But if the other banks find their balances with the Central Bank reduced from £30,000,000 to £26,000,000, their reserves will have been reduced from £80,000,000 to £76,000,000. A strictly proportional reduction of deposits would bring their demand liabilities down to £760,000,000. Even if the reduction is much less drastic than this it may still be sufficient to cause a most palpable set-back to trade. If the Government kept its balances with some bank or banks other than the Central Bank, then its £5,000,000 would be included in the total of £800,000,000 of deposits, and an increase in its balance from £5,000,000 to £10,000,000 would do nothing more than take another £5,000,000 out of that total.

Thus the position of the Government banking account at the Central Bank brings it into direct contact with the nervous system of the money market. A clumsy movement jostling this sensitive organism may occasion spasmodic reactions in the money market which will interfere seriously with the course of trade. Of course, the source of disturbance is the increase of the Government balances *above* the usual level. For reasons of practical convenience balances cannot be allowed to fall to nothing, and there must be some regular system of replenishing them by means of temporary borrowing whenever they are dangerously depleted. An exceptionally small balance is therefore a transient phenomenon which hardly has time to affect the money market before it is past. A large balance, however, may remain undiminished for a considerable time. And when its full effect on the money market has been worked out it may be reduced again by Government disbursements, and cause renewed disturbance. Nevertheless, provided variations of this kind follow a known routine, increasing, for example, at particular seasons of the year, as is usually the case in England, the effect on trade is much diminished, since future changes are discounted beforehand.

In countries where there is no central bank the disposal of Government balances is a problem which is not free from difficulty. In the United States the problem is solved by a compromise, part of the balance being deposited among several of the National Banks, and the remainder being kept by the United States Treasury in its own strong-rooms. The problem happens to be a peculiarly important one in the United States, because it is not the practice there to adjust taxation with any precision year by year to the financial needs of the country. There is in fact no " Budget " at all, and consequently there are alternations of large surpluses and large deficits. The deficits can be met by borrowing, but the disposal of the large surpluses is sometimes the cause of considerable embarrassment. The surpluses accrue during periods of good trade, and therefore of growing inflation. In so far as the money is kept in the Treasury vaults, it is not available for the creation of credit money, and the inflation is to that extent retarded. The question is at what stage the money is to be let loose. The inflation reaches its limit when the quantity of credit money in existence is sufficient to draw all the available legal tender money into circulation. It is at that moment that the money market, in default of a fresh supply of legal tender money, must raise the rate of interest to check the further creation of credit money, and it is at that moment, therefore, that pressure is put on the Government to part with its superfluous funds lest the period of trade activity be brought to an end. The inflation is then increased by the money issued from the Treasury in response to this pressure. Of course, the accumulation of gold in the Treasury will have led to the United States getting more than its proper share of the world's stock of gold, since it must have enough for the ordinary needs of trade in addition to the Treasury balance. And when the Treasury balance is let loose, though there will be some export of the new supply of gold, the inflation will for the moment become greater in the United States than elsewhere. Who flies highest falls furthest, and if the Treasury parts with its gold in this way before the reaction from the state of inflation has begun, it will intensify not only the inflation, but also the subsequent collapse within its own territory. In fact, the practice of accumulating huge hoards of gold places upon the United States Treasury some of the responsibilities of a central bank, but without any of the power which a central bank has of controlling the rate of interest and otherwise regulating its banking operations. Even so something could be done under the system towards the scientific regulation of the money market, if the condition of affairs could be accurately ascertained, and the release of surplus funds carefully delayed until the reaction had clearly begun. It is doubtful, however, whether anything more than a hand-to-mouth policy can be hoped for from the system in practice.

Apart from the regulation of balances, other financial operations on the part of a Government may affect the state of trade. This must especially be the case when there are sudden and great changes in the scale of Government expenditure. The most important example of such changes is to be found in war finance.

On the outbreak of war the belligerent Governments have to enter upon the business of military organisation on a large scale. Military organisation is a business like any other. It includes the provision of both commodities and services. The services are rendered by the soldiers and sailors whose labour is withdrawn from other occupations, and who have to be fed, clothed, and housed like other working-men. The commodities consist of weapons, ships, and other warlike stores. The effective demand for military organisation is created by the compulsory levy of taxes. The sums paid in taxes are withheld from contributing to the effective demand for other commodities and services, and applied to defraying the expenses of Government, including the cost of military organisation. A war compels the Government both to increase the number of soldiers and sailors whose labour is withdrawn from production and to give increased orders for the production of warlike material. The industries of the country may be divided into those in which the demand is increased in this way and those in which it is not. From the former will come a demand for increased loans from the banks to finance the new orders and contracts. For the moment the latter will not be affected (except for some scarcity of labour). The banks will thus experience on the whole an increased demand for borrowed money, and this they will meet by raising the rate of interest. A slackening tendency will then set in in the other trades. The prices of warlike material will rise and the prices of other commodities will tend to fall—more of the former will tend to be imported than before and more of the latter to be exported. All these are the normal consequences of a change in the relative effective demand for different classes of commodities.

But the financing of a war quickly outstrips the reasonable tax-paying capacity of any country, and it is the universal practice to avoid excessive immediate burdens by means of borrowing. The Government enters into the investment market to raise money by pledging its credit. To do so effectively it must offer a rate of interest which, having regard to the security, will be attractive enough to divert the investor from his ordinary course of applying his savings to finance trade. But if the terms are attractive enough to divert the savings of the domestic investor, they will likewise appeal to the foreign investor, who will subscribe to the loans and will then, of course, have to remit money to the belligerent country. This will create a foreign demand for bills of exchange on the belligerent country and the exchange will move to the specie point. Gold will be imported, there will be a corresponding increase in the amount of credit money, and the consequent rise of prices and stimulus to trade will ensue. The high prices will attract imports and divert to domestic consumption goods which would otherwise be exported. An excess of imports will be created, and that (and not

of course the influx of gold) will represent the bulk of
the wealth which is being lent to the belligerent country
from abroad. The money borrowed by the Government
will be spent on military organisation, but it must not
be inferred that the excess of imports will consist wholly
or even mostly of warlike stores. The new imports
may in part be other commodities, the supply of which
sets free part of the productive resources of the country
for military preparations. So long as the country is
borrowing from abroad the additional gold must be
retained, but once the creation of additional credit
money is completed the stimulus to trade will be
exhausted, and when the borrowings from abroad
diminish or cease there must be an export of gold and a
reaction in trade. One of the difficulties in financing
war is that there are several causes combining to raise the
rate of interest just at the time the Government wants
to borrow, and one of these causes is the rise of prices
which occurs as soon as the Government enters the
investment market. To these causes Governments
have frequently added one more potent than any in
the creation of an inconvertible paper currency. When
a nation which already has a metallic currency starts
issuing paper, the mere displacement of the metal by
the paper, apart from the chances of a subsequent
over-issue driving the paper to a discount, of itself
occasions an inflation. For the new notes represent a
clear addition to the world's stock of currency. In 1870
the suspension of specie payments in France drove
great quantities of gold out of the country. There
followed a tendency towards an increase of prices all
over the world which raised the rate of interest just
when France (and Germany, of course, also) wanted to

borrow. Moreover, investors, even if they treat the future purchasing power of gold as an academic question of no interest to them, fully realise the practical importance of the future purchasing power of paper, and they will demand a greater rate of interest if they think it possible that the currency in which the interest is to be paid in future years will be depreciated.

Even the accumulation of a large reserve of gold in a war " chest," only to be used in case of war, is to some extent open to these objections. The sudden issue of a quantity of new gold will cause a rise of prices and a consequent temporary rise in the rate of interest.

Another consequence of war which deserves careful consideration is its effect on credit. War is usually accompanied by a vast destruction of wealth, and the destruction of wealth means the failure of security in the case of the loans charged upon the wealth. The interruption of the ordinary course of trade also will prevent goods from reaching the markets for which they were intended, and deprive them of much of their money value. The expectation that these losses will occur will impair the credit of businesses exposed to the warlike operations. It must not be supposed that even widespread failures on this account will necessarily precipitate a financial crisis and a depression of trade. In the absence of a state of inflation there will be a sufficient supply of gold to build up again the credit money which may have been destroyed through the withholding of credit or through the failure of individual banks. If trade is at the time expanding there will be a pause in its progress ; if it is contracting there will be a momentary hastening of the reaction ; in either case it will resume its course after a brief interval.

But though this applies to the world's trade as a whole, individual countries, and particularly the belligerent countries, may be much more deeply affected. As was explained in Chapter XVI, the impact of any sudden unsettlement of trade falls in the first instance on the investment market, because dealers in investments are largely financed by " day-to-day " loans and "call " loans, instead of by bills maturing at a determinate future date. A complication arises in case of war from the international ramifications of the investment market. As was shown in Chapter X, there are borrowing nations and lending nations, and the great financial houses of the lending nations have connexions all over the world. In the course of their operations these financial houses frequently find themselves with balances in one country or another larger than are necessary for current business. It may often be inconvenient, owing to the state of the exchanges or for other reasons, to remit these surplus funds to headquarters. In that case the money would probably be lent out at call or for short periods to the investment market in the country in which it is deposited, and in the ordinary course it would remain out on these terms until needed for investment in the borrowing country in securities for the issue of which in their own country the lenders have made themselves responsible. If the borrowing country is suddenly exposed to the shock of war, and its material resources subjected to the risk of destruction, the securities representing these material resources in the investment market will be depreciated, and there will at the same time be a further depreciation due to the anticipated or actual competition of Government loans for the available savings. The depreciation will endanger the

loans to the investment market since the collateral
security will be diminished in value, while the outbreak of war may even occasion a loss of confidence in
the facilities for recovering debts in the belligerent
country by the usual civil processes. All these influences combine to induce the lending country to enforce
payment of its short-notice loans, and this may produce
a state of panic in the investment market, which would
inflict heavy losses on the belligerent country. But
the result will be to leave the financiers of the lending
country with large unoccupied balances in the belligerent country. These balances they will not wish
to leave idle, and the alternatives will be either to
remit them home, or to remit them to some other
foreign country, or to invest them on the spot, or after
all to lend them out at call again. Securities having been
driven down to artificially low prices by the forced
realisations consequent upon the calling in of loans, the
belligerent country will have become a very profitable
field of investment, and even if the financiers do not
themselves invest the balances, there will be a tendency
for money to flow from other foreign countries into the
belligerent country, and it will be easy to remit the
balances in the contrary direction. The upshot is that
though the calling in of loans may cause a severe
unsettlement and heavy losses in the belligerent
country, the net effect on the money market, taken as
a whole, will be surprisingly small, for, directly or
indirectly, the money called in will be laid out upon
those very investments which were sold to raise it.

In fact, unlike currency and tariff legislation, war
finance must be classed among those causes which have
less effect than is usually supposed upon the state of

trade. This conclusion must, of course, be interpreted in the light of the narrow significance of the expression " state of trade," with which we are here concerned. While the alternations of good and bad trade are but little modified by the occurrence of great wars, the direct economic loss is none the less for that.

To the several branches of public finance which have engaged our attention in this and in the two preceding chapters it would be possible to add others which have interesting relations with the state of trade, to say nothing of the many economic operations outside the province of Government, which would likewise deserve examination. To attempt to cover the whole ground would be a very formidable task. In any case the answer to the question how fluctuations are caused is to be found rather in the inherent tendency of the existing banking organisations to induce alternate expansions and contractions of credit money, than in these other influences, which hardly do more than modify the primary wave motion.

XX

CAN TRADE FLUCTUATIONS BE PREVENTED ?

IT is not part of my purpose to propose remedies for the mischief traceable to trade fluctuations. But, nevertheless, a brief discussion of the few remedies which have from time to time been proposed for an evil which there seems but little hope of curing will not be out of place. That it is an evil is almost beyond dispute. Capitalists can set the gains of good trade against the losses of bad trade, and it may be that on the whole they do not lose. But the working classes lose both by " good " and by bad trade, and as losses matter much more to people with little wealth than to people with great wealth, the effect (immediate or ultimate) of any economic system on the working classes is the most important test of its expediency. The greater evil, of course, is caused by the periods of bad trade, when not only are the capitalists themselves suffering loss, but the loss which is caused to the working classes takes the peculiarly pernicious form of unemployment. The high prices during good trade mean a diminished command over comforts among the working classes. But unemployment during bad trade concentrates all the loss and misery on the shoulders of a minority whose efficiency, to say nothing of their happiness, may be seriously and permanently impaired.

Remedies for these evils may be divided into two

classes, those which are intended to strike at the root of the evil, and either to prevent the occurrence of fluctuations altogether, or at any rate to mitigate their severity by influencing directly the state of trade, and those which are intended merely to alleviate the evil consequences of a state of things assumed to be inevitable.

In the former class presumably should be placed protective tariffs, the primary purpose of which is to influence trade. We need not cover again the same ground as in Chapter XVIII. It was there shown that it is not the continuance of a protective tariff unchanged, but an increase or decrease which affects the state of trade. Consequently protection will not be of any avail for our present purpose unless an appropriate change could be made in the tariff with every change in the state of trade. Probably to regulate the state of trade by this means would surpass the ingenuity of the ablest Finance Minister, but in any case it is hardly necessary to consider such a proposal seriously, for traders would not acquiesce for a moment in a tariff subject to continual modifications, with all the consequent unsettlement of trade.

I turn next to a proposal which has been advocated by Professor Irving Fisher, and which, though it can hardly at the present time be regarded as within the realm of practical politics, at any rate represents an attempt to base a remedy on a careful diagnosis of the disease. This proposal is for the abandonment of the free coinage of gold with a view to the steadying of the prices of commodities. If the issue and withdrawal of a restricted and overvalued currency, adopted for international use, could be so regulated that the purchasing power of the unit of currency remained absolutely or approximately unchanged, trade fluctuations would be wholly or partly prevented. An excess of credit money would cause a withdrawal of legal tender money instead of an inflation and a rise of prices, while a contraction of credit money would be compensated by a fresh issue of legal tender money. At the same time a steady stream of new legal tender money with the parallel stream of new credit money would automatically provide for the growing population and wealth of the world. In order to carry the plan into operation it would be necessary to establish a central bureau in one of the great commercial countries, which would be responsible for regulating the issues and withdrawals of currency in that country so as to keep the prices of commodities unchanged. All other countries would regulate their own issues and withdrawals of currency by buying and selling exchange upon the monetary centre, at which they would each keep a fund similar in its functions to the fund at present kept by the Indian Government in London. The actual currency used might be overvalued gold, since this would cause the smallest alteration in the habits of nations which at present use gold for purposes of circulation, but inconvertible paper would serve the purpose equally well.[1]

In principle this proposal is thoroughly sound. In practice, however, there are very serious difficulties to face. On the obstacles in the way of arriving at an

---

[1] Professor Fisher proposes that paper convertible into gold, but into a *variable* amount of gold, should be used, the value of the unit of currency being regulated periodically so as to keep the general level of prices as nearly as possible constant.

international agreement for such a purpose there is no
need to dwell. But apart from purely political difficulties, it would be almost impossible to devise a satisfactory method of ascertaining the purchasing power
of the unit of currency. It would be necessary to con-
struct an " Index Number " of the prices of commodities,
which must be based on the prices quoted in important
markets. Such an index number is not a very accurate
measure of the true average of prices. High prices due
to scarcity of individual commodities may increase the
index number and so occasion a withdrawal of currency
just at a time when, if the demand for the deficient
commodities happens to be inelastic, an issue of currency
would be more appropriate. Then prices may be
manipulated by dealers for the deliberate purpose of
affecting the issues of money. And, again, the increase
of a tariff will increase the price of goods duty paid
-and diminish the price *less* duty. No doubt many
other practical difficulties of the same kind might be
found, though it must be recognised that they are
rather in the nature of imperfections in the system
than of organic defects which would destroy its utility.

Perhaps a more serious objection is to be found in
the fact that fluctuations, though they might be
mitigated, would by no means be avoided, even with a
satisfactory measure of purchasing power. It would be
perfectly possible for inflation to occur. If at any
moment there is a shortage of money, there will be an
issue of legal tender money, and the banks will lend
more readily and create fresh credit money. Of course,
as soon as the prescribed average of prices is passed,
there will be withdrawals of legal tender money. But,
just as under the existing regime, the rates of wages

CAN FLUCTUATIONS BE PREVENTED ? 259

will not at once increase in due proportion to the
increased supply of money, and the money market will
arrive at a state of temporary equilibrium with less
than the normal supply of legal tender money and
more than the normal supply of credit money. So long
as this is the case there will be the normal inflated
profits which accompany good trade. But wages will
gradually increase, and as the demand for legal tender
money grows, the rate of interest will be put up and
the supply of credit money will contract, prices will
tend to fall and more legal tender money will be issued.
But prices will only fall so far as wages will permit, and
the new legal tender money is elicited not by a fall in the
stock of money, but by a fall in prices. There would
then be precisely the same deadlock as there is now
when trade is depressed and wages resist the inevitable
fall.

For all that, I think there is a strong presumption
that Professor Irving Fisher's proposal would somewhat reduce, perhaps would greatly reduce, the extent
of the fluctuations. The only question is whether it
would be worth while to face the admitted practical
difficulties, and the possible unforeseen disadvantages,
of the proposal, if it is only to be a palliative and not a
radical cure.

Next we pass to those measures which have been
designed not to prevent or even to mitigate the fluctuations themselves, but to alleviate their consequences.
In the Minority Report of the Poor Law Commission,
issued in 1909, will be found a proposal framed for this
object. It is there suggested (Part II, Chap. V, Recommendation 9) that in order to meet the periodically
recurrent general depression of Trade the Government

should undertake the Regularisation of the National Demand for Labour ; that it should treat a portion of the annual national expenditure upon buildings, stores, etc., to a total amount of about £4,000,000 per annum, as reserved exclusively or mainly for years of depression ; that this programme of expenditure, amounting in the course of a decade to £40,000,000, should be concentrated in those years when the ascertained number of unemployed was above a certain specified limit ; and that the necessary funds should be provided by loan. The underlying principle of this proposal is that the Government should add to the effective demand for labour at the time when the effective demand of private traders falls off. But the writers of the Minority Report appear to have overlooked the fact that the Government by the very fact of borrowing for this expenditure is withdrawing from the investment market savings which would otherwise be applied to the creation of capital. We have had occasion to notice more than once that savings applied to the purchase of securities come to rest sooner or later in a new issue, which will either be the debt of some public body or else will be represented by new fixed capital. If savings to the amount of, say, £10,000,000 are diverted from the creation of capital by a Government loan, the money to be spent by the Government is no doubt increased by that amount, but the money to be spent by private individuals on the construction of fixed capital is correspondingly diminished, at a time when the industries most affected by trade depression are probably those concerned with the construction of fixed capital. It must be conceded that the investments in private concerns are not diminished by the whole amount of the £10,000,000. A certain portion of the national savings will be diverted from investment abroad. But the investment abroad is carried out by the export of goods, and therefore such part of the £10,000,000 as is diverted from foreign investments represents a diminution, not indeed in the construction of fixed capital, but in the output of other industries.

In fact the only beneficial effect which this Government expenditure could have upon the state of employment is to be found in the adjustment of the foreign exchanges necessary to increase the excess of imports (which is normally characteristic of British trade) by the amount by which the net sum sent abroad for investment is diminished, an adjustment so trifling that its practical effects would hardly be discernible at all. Moreover, even if an influx of gold is caused in this way, the gold will only be retained so long as the Government goes on borrowing. If before the depression is over the special expenditure is exhausted and the borrowing slackens or ceases the gold will go abroad again, and the good it did, negligible as it is, will be cancelled by an equally negligible reaction. Indeed, it is needless to labour the point. Once it is shown that the Government expenditure represents an effective demand for labour, not newly created, but diverted from other channels, the proposal of the minority of the Royal Commission (together with many similar proposals supported by less august authority) loses its plausibility.[1]

---

[1] The objections to the proposal are not affected if the money is raised by taxation instead of by loan. To understand this it is necessary to have a clear idea of the position of Government expenditure in the economic organisation of society. As shown in Chapter II, the aggregate effective demand of the community for commodities and the aggregate cost of production of the commodities are equal to one another

Another proposal (which has already been actually carried into partial effect in the United Kingdom by Part II of the National Insurance Act, 1911) is that of compulsory insurance against unemployment. This is based on no theory of economics ; it is quite frankly an attempt to mitigate the distress arising from unemployment. It is to some extent open to the criticism that the funds which it distributes in unemployed benefit are withdrawn from the labour market, since the Insurance fund must meet exceptional calls upon it either by borrowing or by selling securities. But the benefit paid being something far less than full wages, the number of workmen relieved by the receipt of benefit from the most pressing needs will be several times greater than the number who lose employment by the diversion of the money.

If all these proposals amount to so little, it may be asked, is there nothing to be said as to the lines on which a remedy might be sought ? I do not think that there is much. At the same time there certainly are links in the chain of causation which are up to a point within human control. For one thing, it is not impossible that the control of the money market through

and to the aggregate income of the community. The services of Government may be regarded as one class of commodities, the effective demand for which is provided by the compulsory levy of taxation, while the cost of production is made up of the incomes of all the people engaged directly or indirectly in the service of the Government./ The effective demand for all other commodities is made up of the incomes of all members of the community (including those in the service of the Government) less the amount paid in taxation, and the cost of production of all these commodities is made up of the incomes of all people not directly or indirectly in the service of the Government. An increase of Government expenditure diminishes the effective demand for commodities, and diminishes correspondingly the number of people employed in producing commodities.

banking organisation could be improved. If the great central banks of the world, in whose hands this control rests, could agree together to draw the reins a little tighter at times when an expansion of trade is in progress, they might prevent the inflation of credit money reaching the dangerous point. To carry this policy through successfully, they would have to realise that, when the supply of credit money is being increased, *future* demands for cash are being set in motion, and that a margin of reserve ought to be kept in hand to meet those demands when they materialise. And on the other hand, when the supply of credit money is being diminished the banks ought to be in a position to release a sufficient amount of cash to provide for the payment of wages bills on a scale more than proportionate to the aggregate of credit money, since the rate of wages will ultimately fall, and they will then get back the extra cash into their vaults. In practice this would mean that the central banks would maintain a larger proportion of reserves to liabilities than the average when trade is good and a smaller proportion when trade is bad. How much larger and how much smaller could only be settled by experience. And probably no possible precision of judgment would enable the banks to counteract fluctuations altogether. The mere tendency of any casual divergence of the market rate of interest from the profit rate to grow greater and greater until active steps are taken to correct the error would be a perpetual source of minor fluctuations.

But, however efficacious such a method might be, it could hardly be carried into operation so long as the banking system of the United States labours under its existing defects. The central banks of the great com-

mercial nations of Europe might easily unite in any
policy which they all agree to be for the public benefit.
But there is no central bank in the United States.
Moreover, several different circumstances combine to
magnify the importance of the United States in the
monetary system of the world. The material wealth of
a nation of 90,000,000 people inhabiting a vast country
of immeasurable natural resources is on a prodigious
scale. An economic disturbance originating in such a
country causes correspondingly greater perturbations
in the trade of the world than one which takes its rise
within the more modest boundaries of a European
State. And this mere quantitative importance of the
United States in the world's trade is exaggerated in
turn by the chance that makes that country the most
conspicuous devotee of high protection. The high
tariff diminishes the purchasing power of money and,
great as is the material wealth of the United States,
the stock of gold necessary to finance it is greater in
proportion even than in the protectionist states of
Europe. Trade fluctuations in the United States
reverberate throughout the world ; the efflux or influx
of gold is on so great a scale as to dominate all other
money markets.

And yet, as we have seen, the United States has as
unsound a banking system as could well be devised, a
system which might have been planned by a perverse
ingenuity for the express purpose of causing violent
oscillations of trade. Clearly it would be no use for
the great banks of Europe to combine together to
control trade fluctuations if the 20,000 banks of the
United States are to continue blindly building up vast
inflations of credit money, only to land themselves every

few years in a crisis accompanied by the suspension of cash payments and followed by a collapse of industry.

There is, indeed, one method by which any country can practically isolate itself from the effects of a trade disturbance originating abroad. We found in Chapter VIII that the consequences of such a disturbance are hardly felt at all by a country with an independent inconvertible paper currency. That any country should dream of abandoning the existing international standard of value on such grounds sounds impossible. And, of course, it would be futile unless over-issues of the paper money were carefully guarded against, and unless a system of banking control could be devised which would effectively prevent fluctuations being generated in the country itself. But if such a system could be devised, it is quite arguable that it would be worth while to take this course and not to await the establishment of a new conventional international standard in place of gold. A common standard of value is a convenience in international trade, but it is by no means indispensable. It is not very profitable, however, to pursue this subject further, since the possibility of preventing fluctuations by means of banking control is at the best highly conjectural.

Another line of attack upon the problem is through adjustments of wages. In a sense all the mischief of trade fluctuations arises from the tendency of changes in wages to lag behind changes in the value of money. The unemployment during bad trade is mainly the consequence of wages remaining on a level too high for the reduced stock of money. The fall of real wages during good trade is the consequence of delay in the increase of money wages corresponding to the increase in the stock of money. If the working classes would accept an early reduction of wages when a period of bad trade begins and if the employers would give an early increase of wages when a period of good trade begins, not only would the harmful consequences of a trade fluctuation be avoided, but the fluctuation itself might even be prevented. For if an increase or decrease of credit money promptly brought with it a proportionate increase or decrease in the demands for cash, the banks would no longer either drift intó a state of inflation or be led to carry the corresponding process of contraction unnecessarily far.

The obstacle in the way of this plan is that employers and workmen do not trust one another enough to make concessions which are ostensibly temporary, but which they fear may become permanent. The workmen who have accepted a decrease of wages when trade is bad may find difficulty in gaining an increase later on when trade improves. The employers who have granted an increase when trade is good may find difficulty in effecting a decrease when trade slackens again. It is difficult to make either concession conditional on the one which is to follow, for the circumstances in which the latter is to become due are too vague to be easily defined, and in the absence of a definite two-sided bargain, every future proposal for a change of wages will have to be settled on its merits and made the subject, if necessary, of an open dispute.

Something can be done by means of " sliding scales," under which wages in a trade vary to some extent with the prices of the finished products of the trade. But it would be very difficult to devise really effective scales in all trades or even in the majority. And workmen are suspicious of sliding scales, lest employers should regard them as settling the wages question for all time. A sliding scale may easily become obsolete ; for example, new labour-saving apparatus may permanently cheapen the product ; and if sliding scales are ever to be widely adopted this must be recognised.

I will conclude by summarising the essential steps of my argument as briefly as I can.

I. A Depression of Trade occurs when the amount of credit money in existence is more than the bankers think prudent, having regard to their holdings of cash, and they raise the rate of interest in order to reduce the excess.

(1) The rise in the rate of interest increases the cost of holding stocks of commodities, and dealers accordingly proceed to reduce their stocks by giving fewer orders to the producers.

(2) The producers are compelled to reduce their output, except in so far as they can accept orders at lower wholesale prices by sacrificing their profits.

(3) The dealers with their diminished stocks and the producers with their diminished output borrow less money from the banks.

(4) Thus the diminution in the excess of credit money begins, but this involves diminished balances in the control of the community generally and consequently diminished purchases of goods.

(5) The diminished retail demand causes the dealers' stocks to increase again, and the dealers still further diminish their orders to the producers, who in turn borrow still less from the banks.

(6) The restriction of output by the producers throws a portion of the working population out of employment.

(7) The loss of employment affords an inducement to the workmen to accept lower wages.

(8) As wages fall wholesale prices fall, and as wholesale prices fall the dealers are enabled to reduce their retail prices.

(9) As retail prices fall the retail demand for commodities increases, and the wholesale demand increases correspondingly, so that as wages fall output increases and employment improves.

(10) As prices fall the money value of goods in stock or in course of manufacture diminishes, and the borrowings from the banks are not increased on account of the increasing output.

(11) When the excess of credit money has been completely removed the banks no longer need to keep up the rate of interest. The rate of interest is then reduced to the " profit rate," and the deterrent effect upon holding stocks of goods ceases.

(12) At this stage part of the labour and capital of the community are still unemployed, and therefore to complete a return to normal conditions it would be necessary for wages and prices to fall further.

II. An Expansion of Trade occurs when the amount of credit money in existence is less than the bankers think prudent, having regard to their holdings of cash, and they lower the rate of interest in order to encourage borrowing.

(1) The fall in the rate of interest diminishes the

cost of holding stocks of commodities, and dealers increase their orders to the producers.

(2) The producers increase their output and raise wholesale prices.

(3) Both dealers and producers borrow more money from the banks.

(4) The amount of credit money is increased, and purchases of goods are increased correspondingly.

(5) The increased retail demand depletes the stocks of commodities and the dealers still further increase their orders to the producers, who in turn borrow still more from the banks.

(6) The increase of output causes an abnormal demand for labour.

(7) The abnormal demand for labour gives the workmen an opportunity to claim higher wages.

(8) Output cannot be increased indefinitely and the dealers have to raise retail prices to protect their stocks against the growing retail demand.

(9) As prices rise the money value of goods in stock or in course of manufacture increases and borrowings from the banks are still further increased.

(10) When the deficiency of credit money has been completely filled up the banks no longer need to keep down the rate of interest. The rate of interest is then raised to the " profit rate," and the inducement to increase stocks of goods is removed.

(11) At this stage money wages have not yet

increased in proportion to prices, and to complete a return to normal conditions a further increase in money wages is necessary.

III. Trade Depressions tend to be followed by Trade Expansions, and Trade Expansions in turn by Trade Depressions.

(1) The banks limit the creation of credit money according to the consequent demands upon them for cash.

(2) The most important item in the community's demand for cash is the wages bill.

(3) When a trade expansion is in progress the increase in the wages bill of the community follows the increase in the amount of credit money at a considerable interval.

(4) The banks are able, therefore, without immediately causing excessive demands for cash, to increase credit money to an amount which will ultimately overtax the available stock of cash.

(5) At a time when an expansion of trade is in progress the rate of interest (though below the profit rate) is so high that imprudent banking is profitable, and unless the danger is foreseen and provided against this excessive creation of credit money will occur.

(6) When the corresponding demands for cash actually arise the excess of credit money has to be reduced, and all the phenomena of a trade depression ensue.

(7) The same arguments apply *mutatis mutandis* to a trade depression, for in that case the decrease in the

wages bill of the community follows the decrease in credit money at a considerable interval.

(8) The bankers reduce credit money to a level which will ultimately keep in circulation less than the available stock of cash.

(9) During a depression the rate of interest (though above the profit rate) is too low to stimulate the banks to push their business.

(10) By the time the fall of wages consequent on the depression has made substantial progress the banks find superfluous accumulations of cash in their vaults ; they take steps to increase credit money again and all the phenomena of a trade expansion ensue.

IV. If at any time trade happened to be steady any casual disturbance tends to be magnified.

(1) If the disturbance is a casual increase in the amount of credit money the increase tends to cause a rise of prices, an increase in the profit rate, and a further increase in the amount of credit money, until the process is checked by a rise in the rate of interest.

(2) If the disturbance is a casual decrease in the amount of credit money the decrease tends to cause a fall in prices, a decrease in the profit rate, and a future decrease in the amount of credit money, until the process is checked by a fall in the rate of interest.

(3) Thus even if the state of trade ever became perfectly steady, there would be an element of instability in it which would make the first casual disturbance the starting-point of a new series of fluctuations.

It will be observed that the foregoing summary does not cover all the points previously discussed. It includes, however, those which form part of the main stream of argument. The real starting-point of the whole is to be found in the thesis (which few, I imagine, will be found to dispute) that a depression of trade is in essence a general slackening of the money demand for commodities, and an expansion of trade is a general augmentation of the money demand for commodities. All the rest merely traces the causes and consequences of these variations in demand.

INDEX